A PERSONAL RECORD

JOSEPH CONRAD

A PERSONAL RECORD

AFTERWORD BY ALBERT J. GUERARD

THE MARLBORO PRESS
MARLBORO, VERMONT
1988

Library of Congress Catalog Card Number 88-60728

ISBN 0-910395-46-2

Manufactured in the United States of America

CONTENTS

A PERSONAL RECORD

A FAMILIAR PREFACE

A S a general rule we do not want much encourage-
ment to talk about ourselves; yet this little book is
the result of a friendly suggestion, and even of a little
friendly pressure. I defended myself with some spirit; but,
with characteristic tenacity, the friendly voice insisted,
"You know, you really must."

It was not an argument, but I submitted at once. If one
must! . . .

You perceive the force of the word. He who wants to
persuade should put his trust not in the right argument,
but in the right word. The power of sound has always
been greater than the power of sense. I don't say this by
way of disparagement. It is better for mankind to be im-
pressionable than reflective. Nothing humanly great—
great, I mean, as affecting a whole mass of lives—has
come from reflection. On the other hand, you cannot fail
to see the power of mere words; such words as Glory, for
instance, or Pity. I won't mention any more. They are not
far to seek. Shouted with perseverance, with ardor, with
conviction, thee two by their sound alone have set whole
nations in motion and upheaved the dry, hard ground on
which rests our whole social fabric. There's "virtue" for
you if you like! . . . Of course the accent must be attended

1

to. The right accent. That's very important. The capacious lung, the thundering or the tender vocal chords. Don't talk to me of your Archimedes' lever. He was an absent-minded person with a mathematical imagination. Mathematics commands all my respect, but I have no use for engines. Give me the right word and the right accent and I will move the world.

What a dream for a writer! Because written words have their accent too. Yes! Let me only find the right word! Surely it must be lying somewhere among the wreckage of all the plaints and all the exultations poured out aloud since the first day when hope, the undying, came down on earth. It may be there, close by, disregarded, invisible, quite at hand. But it's no good. I believe there are men who can lay hold of a needle in a pottle of hay at the first try. For myself, I have never had such luck.

And then there is that accent. Another difficulty. For who is going to tell whether the accent is right or wrong till the word is shouted, and fails to be heard, perhaps, and goes down-wind, leaving the world unmoved? Once upon a time there lived an emperor who was a sage and something of a literary man. He jotted down on ivory tablets thoughts, maxims, reflections which chance has preserved for the edification of posterity. Among other sayings—I am quoting from memory—I remember this solemn admonition: "Let all thy words have the accent of heroic truth." The accent of heroic truth! This is very fine, but I am thinking that it is an easy matter for an austere emperor to jot down grandiose advice. Most of the working truths on this earth are humble, not heroic: and there have been times in the history of mankind when the accents of heroic truth have moved it to nothing but derision.

Nobody will expect to find between the covers of this little book words of extraordinary potency or accents of irresistible heroism. However humiliating for my self-esteem, I must confess that the counsels of Marcus Aurelius are not for me. They are more fit for a moralist than for an artist. Truth of a modest sort I can promise you, and also sincerity. That complete, praiseworthy sincerity which, while it delivers one into the hands of one's enemies, is as likely as not to embroil one with one's friends.

"Embroil" is perhaps too strong an expression. I can't imagine among either my enemies or my friends a being so hard up for something to do as to quarrel with me. "To disappoint one's friends" would be nearer the mark. Most, almost all, friendships of the writing period of my life have come to me through my books; and I know that a novelist lives in his work. He stands there, the only reality in an invented world, among imaginary things, happenings, and people. Writing about them, he is only writing about himself. But the disclosure is not complete. He remains, to a certain extent, a figure behind the veil; a suspected rather than a seen presence—a movement and a voice behind the draperies of fiction. In these personal notes there is no such veil. And I cannot help thinking of a passage in the *Imitation of Christ* where the ascetic author, who knew life so profoundly, says that "there are persons esteemed on their reputation who by showing themselves destroy the opinion one had of them." This is the danger incurred by an author of fiction who sets out to talk about himself without disguise.

While these reminiscent pages were appearing serially I was remonstrated with for bad economy; as if such writing were a form of self-indulgence wasting the substance of future volumes. It seems that I am not sufficiently literary. Indeed, a man who never wrote a line for print till he was thirty-six cannot bring himself to look upon his existence and his experience, upon the sum of his thoughts, sensations, and emotions, upon his memories and his regrets, and the whole possession of his past, as only so much material for his hands. Once before, some three years ago, when I published *The Mirror of the Sea*, a volume of impressions and memories, the same remarks

3

were made to me. Practical remarks. But, truth to say, I have never understood the kind of thrift they recommend. I wanted to pay my tribute to the sea, its ships and its men, to whom I remain indebted for so much which has gone to make me what I am. That seemed to me the only shape in which I could offer it to their shades. There could not be a question in my mind of anything else. It is quite possible that I am a bad economist; but it is certain that I am incorrigible.

Having matured in the surroundings and under the special conditions of sea life, I have a special piety toward that form of my past; for its impressions were vivid, its appeal direct, its demands such as could be responded to with the natural elation of youth and strength equal to the call. There was nothing in them to perplex a young conscience. Having broken away from my origins under a storm of blame from every quarter which had the merest shadow of right to voice an opinion, removed by great distances from such natural affections as were still left to me, and even estranged, in a mesure, from them by the totally unintelligible character of the life which had seduced me so mysteriously from my allegiance, I may safely say that through the blind force of circumstances the sea was to be all my world and the merchant service my only home for a long succession of years. No wonder, then, that in my two exclusively sea books—*The Nigger of the Narcissus* and *The Mirror of the Sea* (and in a few short stories like "Youth" and "Typhoon")—I have tried with an almost filial regard to render the vibration of life in the great world of waters, in the hearts of the simple men who have for ages traversed its solitudes, and also that something sentient which seems to dwell in ships— the creatures of their hands and the objects of their care.

One's literary life must turn frequently for sustenance to memories and seek discourse with the shades, unless one has made up one's mind to write only in order to reprove mankind for what it is, or praise it for what it is

4

not, or—generally—to teach it how to behave. Being neither quarrelsome, nor a flatterer, nor a sage, I have done
none of these things, and I am prepared to put up serenely
with the insignificance which attaches to persons who
are not meddlesome in some way or another. But resignation is not indifference. I would not like to be left
standing as a mere spectator on the bank of the great
stream carrying onward so many lives. I would fain claim
for myself the faculty of so much insight as can be expressed in a voice of sympathy and compassion.

It seems to me that in one, at least, authoritative quarter of criticism I am suspected of a certain unemotional,
grim acceptance of facts—of what the French would call
sécheresse du cœur. Fifteen years of unbroken silence
before praise or blame testify sufficiently to my respect
for criticism, that fine flower of personal expression in
the garden of letters. But this is more of a personal matter,
reaching the man behind the work, and therefore it may
be alluded to in a volume which is a personal note in the
margin of the public page. Not that I feel hurt in the least.
The charge—if it amounted to a charge at all—was made
in the most considerate terms; in a tone of regret.

My answer is that if it be true that every novel contains
an element of autobiography—and this can hardly be de-
nied, since the creator can only express himself in his
creation—then there are some of us to whom an open
display of sentiment is repugnant. I would not unduly
praise the virtue of restraint. It is often merely tempera-
mental. But it is not always a sign of coldness. It may be
pride. There can be nothing more humiliating than to see
the shaft of one's emotion miss the mark of either laughter or tears. Nothing more humiliating! And this for the
reason that should the mark be missed, should the open
display of emotion fail to move, then it must perish un-
avoidably in disgust or contempt. No artist can be re-
proached for shrinking from a risk which only fools run to
meet and only genius dare confront with impunity. In a

5

task which mainly consists in laying one's soul more or less bare to the world, a regard for decency, even at the cost of success, is but the regard for one's own dignity which is inseparably united with the dignity of one's work.

And then—it is very difficult to be wholly joyous or wholly sad on this earth. The comic, when it is human, soon takes upon itself a face of pain; and some of our griefs (some only, not all, for it is the capacity for suffering which makes man august in the eyes of men) have their sources in weaknesses which must be recognized with smiling compassion as the common inheritance of us all. Joy and sorrow in this world pass into each other, mingling their forms and their murmurs in the twilight of life as mysterious as an overshadowed ocean, while the dazzling brightness of supreme hopes lies far off, fascinating and still, on the distant edge of the horizon.

Yes! I too would like to hold the magic wand giving that command over laughter and tears which is declared to be the highest achievement of imaginative literature. Only, to be a great magician one must surrender oneself to occult and irresponsible powers, either outside or within one's breast. We have all heard of simple men selling their souls for love or power to some grotesque devil. The most ordinary intelligence can perceive without much reflection that anything of the sort is bound to be a fool's bargain. I don't lay claim to particular wisdom because of my dislike and distrust of such transactions. It may be my sea training acting upon a natural disposition to keep good hold on the one thing really mine, but the fact is that I have a positive horror of losing even for one moving moment that full possession of myself which is the first condition of good service. And I have carried my notion of good service from my earlier into my later existence. I, who have never sought in the written word anything else but a form of the Beautiful—I have carried over that article of creed from the decks of ships to the more circumscribed space of my desk, and by that act, I suppose, I have become permanently imperfect in the eyes of the ineffable company of pure esthetes.

As in political so in literary action a man wins friends for himself mostly by the passion of his prejudices and by the consistent narrowness of his outlook. But I have never been able to love what was not lovable or hate what was not hateful out of deference for some general principle. Whether there be any courage in making this admission I know not. After the middle turn of life's way we consider dangers and joys with a tranquil mind. So I proceed in peace to declare that I have always suspected in the effort to bring into play the extremities of emotions the debasing touch of insincerity. In order to move others deeply we must deliberately allow ourselves to be carried away beyond the bounds of our normal sensibility—innocently enough, perhaps, and of necessity, like an actor who raises his voice on the stage above the pitch of natural conversation—but still we have to do that. And surely this is no great sin. But the danger lies in the writer becoming the victim of his own exaggeration, losing the exact notion of sincerity, and in the end coming to despise truth itself as something too cold, too blunt for his purpose—as, in fact, not good enough for his insistent emotion. From laughter and tears the descent is easy to sniveling and giggles.

These may seem selfish considerations; but you can't, in sound morals, condemn a man for taking care of his own integrity. It is his clear duty. And least of all can you condemn an artist pursuing, however humbly and imperfectly, a creative aim. In that interior world where his thought and his emotions go seeking for the experience of imagined adventures, there are no policemen, no law, no pressure of circumstance or dread of opinion to keep him within bounds. Who then is going to say Nay to his temptations if not his own conscience?

And besides—this, remember, is the place and the moment of perfectly open talk—I think that all ambitions are lawful except those which climb upward on the miseries or the credulities of mankind. All intellectual and artistic ambitions are permissible, up to and even beyond the limit of prudent sanity. They can hurt no one. If they are mad, then so much the worse for the artist. Indeed, as virtue is said to be, such ambitions are their own reward. Is it such a very mad presumption to believe in the sovereign power of one's art, to try for other means, for other ways of affirming this belief in the deeper appeal of one's work? To try to go deeper is not to be insensible. A historians of hearts is not a historian of emotions, yet he penetrates further, restrained as he may be, since his aim is to reach the very fount of laughter and tears. The sight of human affairs deserves admiration and pity. They are worthy of respect, too. And he is not insensible who pays them the undemonstrative tribute of a sigh which is not a sob, and of a smile which is not a grin. Resignation, not mystic, not detached, but resignation open-eyed, conscious, and informed by love, is the only one of our feelings for which it is impossible to become a sham.

Not that I think resignation the last word of wisdom. I am too much the creature of my time for that. But I think that the proper wisdom is to will what the gods will without, perhaps, being certain what their will is—or even if they have a will of their own. And in this matter of life and art it is not the Why that matters so much to our happiness as the How. As the Frenchman said, "*Il y a toujours la manière.*" Very true. Yes. There is the manner. The manner in laughter, in tears, in irony, in indignations and enthusiasms, in judgments—and even in love. The manner in which, as in the features and character of a human face, the inner truth is foreshadowed for those who know how to look at their kind.

Those who read me know my conviction that the world, the temporal world, rests on a few very simple ideas; so simple that they must be as old as the hills. It rests notably, among others, on the idea of Fidelity. At a time when nothing which is not revolutionary in some way or other can expect to attract much attention I have not been revolutionary in my writings. The revolutionary spirit is mighty convenient in this, that it frees one from all scruples as regards ideas. Its hard, absolute optimism is repulsive to my mind by the menace of fanaticism and intolerance it contains. No doubt one should smile at these things; but, imperfect Esthete, I am no better Philosopher. All claim to special righteousness awakens in me that scorn and danger from which a philosophical mind should be free. . . .

I fear that trying to be conversational I have only managed to be unduly discursive. I have never been very well acquainted with the art of conversation—that art which, I understand, is supposed to be lost now. My young days, the days when one's habits and character are formed, have been rather familiar with long silences. Such voices as broke into them were anything but conversational. No. I haven't got the habit. Yet this discursiveness is not so irrelevant to the handful of pages which follow. They, too, have been charged with discursiveness, with disregard of chronological order (which is in itself a crime), with unconventionality of form (which is an impropriety). I was told severely that the public would view with displeasure the informal character of my recollections. "Alas!" I protested, mildly. "Could I begin with the sacramental words, 'I was born on such a date in such a place'? The remoteness of the locality would have robbed the statement of all interest. I haven't lived through wonderful adventures to be related *seriatim*. I haven't known distinguished men on whom I could pass fatuous remarks. I haven't been mixed up with great or scandalous affairs. This is but a bit of psychological document, and even so, I haven't written it with a view to put forward any conclusion of my own."

But my objector was not placated. These were good

reasons for not writing at all—not a defense of what stood written already, he said.

I admit that almost anything, anything in the world, would serve as a good reason for not writing at all. But since I have written them, all I want to say in their defense is that these memories put down without any regard for established conventions have not been thrown off without system and purpose. They have their hope and their aim. The hope that from the reading of these pages there may emerge at last the vision of a personality; the man behind the books so fundamentally dissimilar as, for instance, *Almayer's Folly* and *The Secret Agent*, and yet a coherent, justifiable personality both in its origin and in its action. This is the hope. The immediate aim, closely associated with the hope, is to give the record of personal memories by presenting faithfully the feelings and sensations connected with the writing of my first book and with my first contact with the sea.

In the purposely mingled resonance of this double strain a friend here and there will perhaps detect a subtle accord.

J. C. K.

I

BOOKS may be written in all sorts of places. Verbal inspiration may enter the berth of a mariner on board a ship frozen fast in a river in the middle of a town; and since saints are supposed to look benignantly on humble believers, I indulge in the pleasant fancy that the shade of old Flaubert—who imagined himself to be (amongst other things) a descendant of Vikings—might have hovered with amused interest over the decks of a 2,000-ton steamer called the *Adowa*, on board of which, gripped by the inclement winter alongside a quay in Rouen, the tenth chapter of *Almayer's Folly* was begun. With interest, I say, for was not the kind Norman giant with enormous mustaches and a thundering voice the last of the Romantics? Was he not, in his unworldly, almost ascetic, devotion to his art, a sort of literary, saint-like hermit?

"It has set at last,' said Nina to her mother, pointing to the hills behind which the sun had sunk." ... These words of Almayer's romantic daughter I remember tracing on the grey paper of a pad which rested on the blanket of my bed-place. They referred to a sunset in Malayan Isles, and shaped themselves in my mind, in a hallucinated vision of forests and rivers and seas, far removed from a commercial and yet romantic town of the northern

11

hemisphere. But at that moment the mood of visions and words was cut short by the third officer, a cheerful and casual youth, coming in with a bang of the door and the exclamation: "You've made it jolly warm in here."

It was warm. I had turned on the steam-heater after placing a tin under the leaky water-cock—for perhaps you do not know that water will leak where steam will not. I am not aware of what my young friend had been doing on deck all that morning, but the hands he rubbed together vigorously were very red and imparted to me a chilly feeling by their mere aspect. He has remained the only banjoist of my acquaintance, and being also a younger son of a retired colonel, the poem of Mr. Kipling, by a strange aberration of associated ideas, always seems to me to have been written with an exclusive view to his person. When he did not play the banjo he loved to sit and look at it. He proceeded to this sentimental inspection, and after meditating a while over the strings under my silent scrutiny, inquired airily:

"What are you always scribbling there, if it's fair to ask?"

It was a fair enough question, but I did not answer him, and simply turned the pad over with a movement of instinctive secrecy: I could not have told him he had put to flight the psychology of Nina Almayer, her opening speech of the tenth chapter and the words of Mrs. Almayer's wisdom which were to follow in the ominous oncoming of a tropical night. I could not have told him that Nina had said: "It has set at last." He would have been extremely surprised and perhaps have dropped his precious banjo. Neither could I have told him that the sun of my sea-going was setting too, even as I wrote the words expressing the impatience of passionate youth bent on its desire. I did not know this myself, and it is safe to say he would not have cared, though he was an excellent young fellow and treated me with more deference than, in our relative positions, I was strictly entitled to.

He lowered a tender gaze on his banjo, and I went on looking through the port-hole. The round opening framed in its brass rim a fragment of the quays, with a row of casks ranged on the frozen ground and the tail-end of a great cart. A red-nosed carter in a blouse and a woollen night-cap leaned against the wheel. An idle, strolling custom-house guard, belted over his blue *capote*, had the air of being depressed by exposure to the weather and the monotony of official existence. The background of grimy houses found a place in the picture framed by my port-hole, across a wide stretch of paved quay, brown with frozen mud. The colouring was somber, and the most conspicuous feature was a little café with curtained windows and a shabby front of white woodwork, corresponding with the squalor of these poorer quarters bordering the river. We had been shifted down there from another berth in the neighborhood of the Opera House, where that same port-hole gave me a view of quite another sort of café—the best in the town, I believe, and the very one where the worthy Bovary and his wife, the romantic daughter of old Père Renault, had some refreshment after the memorable performance of an opera which was the tragic story of Lucia di Lammermoor in a setting of light music.

I could recall no more the hallucination of the Eastern Archipelago which I certainly hoped to see again. The story of *Almayer's Folly* got put away under the pillow for that day. I do not know that I had any occupation to keep me away from it; the truth of the matter is that on board that ship we were leading just then a contemplative life. I will not say anything of my privileged position. I was there "just to oblige," as an actor of standing may take a small part in the benefit performance of a friend.

As far as my feelings were concerned, I did not wish to be in that steamer at that time and in those circumstances. And perhaps I was not even wanted there in the usual sense in which a ship "wants" an officer. It was the

13

first and last instance in my sea life when I served ship-owners who have remained completely shadowy to my apprehension. I do not mean this for the well-known firm of London ship-brokers which had chartered the ship to the, I will not say short-lived, but ephemeral Franco-Canadian Transport Company. A death leaves something behind, but there was never anything tangible left from the F.C.T.C. It flourished no longer than roses live, and unlike the roses, it blossomed in the dead of winter, emitted a sort of faint perfume of adventure, and died before spring set in. But indubitably it was a company, it even had a house-flag, all white with the letters F.C.T.C. artfully tangled up in a complicated monogram. We flew it at our mainmast head, and now I have come to the conclusion that it was the only flag of its kind in existence. All the same, we on board, for many days, had the impression of being a unit of a large fleet with fortnightly departures for Montreal and Quebec as advertised in pamphlets and prospectuses which came aboard in a large package in Victoria Dock, London, just before we started for Rouen, France. And in the shadow life of the F.C.T.C. lies the secret of that, my last employment in my calling, which in a remote sense interrupted the rhythmical development of Nina Almayer's story.

The then secretary of the London Shipmasters' Society, with its modest rooms in Fenchurch Street, was a man of indefatigable activity and the greatest devotion to his task. He is responsible for what was my last association with a ship. I called it that because it can hardly be called a sea-going experience. Dear Captain Froud—it is impossible not to pay him the tribute of affectionate familiarity at this distance of years—had very sound views as to the advancement of knowledge and status for the whole body of the officers of the mercantile marine. He organized for us courses of professional lectures, St. John ambulance classes, corresponded industriously with public bodies and members of Parliament on subjects touching the interests of the service; and as to the oncoming of some inquiry or commission relating to matters of the sea and to the work of seamen, it was a perfect godsend to his need of exerting himself on our corporate behalf. Together with this high sense of his official duties he had in him a vein of personal kindness, a strong disposition to do what good he could to the individual members of that craft of which in his time he had been a very excellent master. And what greater kindness can one do to a seaman than to put him in the way of employment? Captain Froud did not see why the Shipmasters' Society, besides its general guardianship of our interests, should not be unofficially an employment agency of the very highest class.

"I am trying to persuade all our great ship-owning firms to come to us for their men. There is nothing of a trade-union spirit about our society, and I really don't see why they should not," he said once to me. "I am always telling the captains, too, that all things being equal they ought to give preference to the members of the society. In my position I can generally find for them what they want among our members or our associate members."

In my wanderings about London from west to east and back again (I was very idle then), the two little rooms in Fenchurch Street were a sort of resting-place where my spirit, hankering after the sea, could feel itself nearer to the ships, the men, and the life of its choice—nearer there than any other spot of the solid earth. This resting-place used to be, at about five o'clock in the afternoon, full of men and tobacco smoke, but Captain Froud had the smaller room to himself and there he granted private interviews, whose principal motive was to render service. Thus, one murky November afternoon, he beckoned me in with a crooked finger and that peculiar glance above his spectacles which is perhaps my strongest physical recollection of the man.

"I have had in here a shipmaster, this morning," he said, getting back to his desk and motioning me to a chair,

15

"who is in want of an officer. It's for a steamship. You know, nothing pleases me more than to be asked, but unfortunately I do not quite see my way . . ."

As the outer room was full of men, I cast a wondering glance at the closed door, but he shook his head.

"Oh yes, I should be only too glad to get that berth for one of them. But the fact of the matter is, the captain of that ship wants an officer who can speak French fluently, and that's not so easy to find. I do not know anybody myself but you. It's a second officer's berth and, of course, you would not care . . . would you now? I know that it isn't what you are looking for."

It was not. I had given myself up to the idleness of a haunted man who looks for nothing but words wherein to capture his visions. But I admit that outwardly I resembled sufficiently a man who could make a second officer for a steamer chartered by a French company. I showed no sign of being haunted by the fate of Nina and by the murmurs of tropical forests; and even my intimate intercourse with Almayer (a person of weak character) had not put a visible mark upon my features. For many years he and the world of his story had been the companions of my imagination without, I hope, impairing my ability to deal with the realities of sea life. I had had the man and his surroundings with me ever since my return from the eastern waters, some four years before the day of which I speak.

It was in the front sitting-room of furnished apartments in a Pimlico square that they first began to live again with a vividness and poignancy quite foreign to our former real intercourse. I had been treating myself to a long stay on shore, and in the necessity of occupying my mornings, Almayer (that old acquaintance) came nobly to the rescue. Before long, as was only proper, his wife and daughter joined him round my table, and then the rest of that Pantai band came full of words and gestures. Unknown to my respectable landlady, it was my practice directly after

16

my breakfast to hold animated receptions of Malays, Arabs and half-castes. They did not clamour aloud for my attention. They came with a silent and irresistible appeal—and the appeal, I affirm here, was not to my self-love or my vanity. It seems now to have had a moral character, for why should the memory of these beings, seen in their obscure, sun-bathed existence, demand to express itself in the shape of a novel, except on the ground of that mysterious fellowship which unites in a community of hopes and fears all the dwellers on this earth?

I did not receive my visitors with boisterous rapture as the bearers of any gifts of profit or fame. There was no vision of a printed book before me as I sat writing at that table, situated in a decayed part of Belgravia. After all these years, each leaving its evidence of slowly blackened pages, I can honestly say that it is a sentiment akin to piety which prompted me to render in words assembled with conscientious care the memory of things far distant and of men who had lived.

But, coming back to Captain Froud and his fixed idea of never disappointing ship-owners or ship-captains, it was not likely that I should fail him in his ambition—to satisfy at a few hours' notice the unusual demand for a French-speaking officer. He explained to me that the ship was chartered by a French company intending to establish a regular monthly line of sailings from Rouen, for the transport of French emigrants to Canada. But, frankly, this sort of thing did not interest me very much. I said gravely that if it were really a matter of keeping up the reputation of the Shipmasters' Society, I would consider it. But the consideration was just for form's sake. The next day I interviewed the captain, and I believe we were impressed favourably with each other. He explained that his chief mate was an excellent man in every respect, and that he could not think of dismissing him so as to give me the higher position; but that if I consented to come as second officer I would be given certain special advantages—and so on.

I told him that if I came at all the rank really did not matter.

"I am sure," he insisted, "you will get on first rate with Mr. Paramor."

I promised faithfully to stay for two trips at least, and it was in those circumstances that what was to be my last connection with a ship began. And after all there was not even one single trip. It may be that it was simply the fulfilment of a fate, of that written word on my forehead which apparently forbade me, through all my sea wanderings, ever to achieve the crossing of the Western Ocean— using the words in that special sense in which sailors speak of Western Ocean trade, of Western Ocean packets, of Western Ocean hard cases. The new life attended closely upon the old, and the nine chapters of *Almayer's Folly* went with me to the Victoria Dock, whence in a few days we started for Rouen. I won't go so far as to say that the engaging of a man fated never to cross the Western Ocean was the absolute cause of the Franco-Canadian Transport Company's failure to achieve even a single passage. It might have been that, of course; but the obvious, gross obstacle was clearly the want of money. Four hundred and sixty bunks for emigrants were put together in the 'tween decks by industrious carpenters while we lay in the Victoria Dock, but never an emigrant turned up in Rouen—of which, being a humane person, I confess I was glad. Some gentlemen from Paris—I think there were three of them, and one was said to be the Chairman— turned up indeed and went from end to end of the ship, knocking their silk hats cruelly against the deck-beams. I attended them personally, and I can vouch for it that the interest they took in things was intelligent enough, though obviously they had never seen anything of the sort before. Their faces as they went ashore wore a cheerfully inconclusive expression. Notwithstanding that this inspecting ceremony was supposed to be a preliminary to immediate sailing, it was then, as they filed down our gangway, that I received the inward monition that no sailing within the meaning of our charter-party would ever take place.

It must be said that in less than three weeks a move took place. When we first arrived we had been taken up with much ceremony well toward the centre of the town, and, all the street corners being placarded with the tri-colour posters announcing the birth of our company, the *petit bourgeois* with his wife and family made a Sunday holiday from the inspection of the ship. I was always in evidence in my best uniform to give information as though I had been a Cook's tourists' interpreter, while our quarter-masters reaped a harvest of small change from personally conducted parties. But when the move was made—that move which carried us some mile and a half down the stream to be tied up to an altogether muddier and shabbier quay—then indeed the desolation of soli-tude became our lot. It was a complete and soundless stagnation; for, as we had the ship ready for sea to the smallest detail, as the frost was hard and the days short, we were absolutely idle—idle to the point of blushing with shame when the thought struck us that all the time our salaries went on. Young Cole was aggrieved because, as he said, we could not enjoy any sort of fun in the evening after loafing like this all day: even the banjo lost its charm since there was nothing to prevent his strum-ming on it all the time between the meals. The good Paramor—he was really a most excellent fellow—became unhappy as far as was possible to his cheery nature, till one dreary day I suggested, out of sheer mischief, that he should employ the dormant energies of the crew in haul-ing both cables up on deck and turning them end for end.

For a moment Mr. Paramor was radiant. "Excellent idea!" but directly his face fell. "Why . . . Yes! But we can't make that job last more than three days," he mut-

19

tered discontentedly. I don't know how long he expected us to be stuck on the river-side outskirts of Rouen, but I know that the cables got hauled up and turned end for end according to my satanic suggestion, put down again, and their very existence utterly forgotten, I believe, before a French river pilot came on board to take our ship down, empty as she came, into the Havre roads. You may think that this state of forced idleness favoured some advance in the fortunes of Almayer and his daughter. Yet it was not so. As if it were some sort of evil spell, my banjoist cabin-mate's interruption, as related above, had arrested them short at the point of that fateful sunset for many weeks together. It was always thus with this book, begun in '89 and finished in '94—with that shortest of all the novels which it was to be my lot to write. Between its opening exclamation calling Almayer to his dinner in his wife's voice and Abdullah's (his enemy) mental reference to the God of Islam—"The Merciful, the Compassionate"—which closes the book, there were to come several long sea passages, a visit (to use the elevated phraseology suitable to the occasion) to the scenes (some of them) of my childhood and the realization of childhood's vain words, expressing a light-hearted and romantic whim.

It was in 1868, when nine years old or thereabouts, that while looking at a map of Africa of the time and putting my finger on the blank space then representing the unsolved mystery of that continent, I said to myself with absolute assurance and an amazing audacity which are no longer in my character now:

"When I grow up I shall go *there*."

And of course I thought no more about it till after a quarter of a century or so an opportunity offered to go there—as if the sin of childish audacity were to be visited on my mature head. Yes. I did go there: *there* being the region of Stanley Falls, which in '68 was the blankest of blank spaces on the earth's figured surface. And the MS.

of *Almayer's Folly*, carried about me as if it were a talis-
man or a treasure, went *there* too. That it ever came out
of *there* seems a special dispensation of Providence; because a good many of my other properties, infinitely more
valuable and useful to me, remained behind through unfortunate accidents of transportation. I call to mind, for
instance, a specially awkward turn of the Congo between
Kinchassa and Leopoldsville—more particularly when
one had to take it at night in a big canoe with only half
the proper number of paddlers. I failed in being the second
white man on record drowned at that interesting spot
through the upsetting of a canoe. The first was a young
Belgian officer, but the accident happened some months
before my time, and he, too, I believe, was going home;
not perhaps quite so ill as myself—but still he was going
home. I got round the turn more or less alive, though I
was too sick to care whether I did or not, and, always with
Almayer's Folly among my diminishing baggage, I arrived
at that delectable capital Boma, where before the departure of the steamer which was to take me home, I had the
time to wish myself dead over and over again with perfect
sincerity. At that date there were in existence only seven
chapters of *Almayer's Folly*, but the chapter in my history
which followed was that of a long, long illness and very
dismal convalescence. Geneva, or more precisely the hy-
dropathic establishment of Champel, is rendered forever
famous by the termination of the eighth chapter in the
history of Almayer's decline and fall. The events of the
ninth are inextricably mixed up with the details of the
proper management of a waterside warehouse owned by a
certain city firm whose name does not matter. But that
work, undertaken to accustom myself again to the activ-
ities of a healthy existence, soon came to an end. The
earth had nothing to hold me with for very long. And then
that memorable story, like a cask of choice Madeira, got
carried for three years to and fro upon the sea. Whether
this treatment improved its flavour or not, of course I

would not like to say. As far as appearance is concerned, it certainly did nothing of the kind. The whole MS. acquired a faded look and an ancient, yellowish complexion. It became at last unreasonable to suppose that anything in the world would ever happen to Almayer and Nina. And yet something most unlikely to happen on the high seas was to wake them up from their state of suspended animation.

What is it that Novalis says? "It is certain my conviction gains infinitely at the moment another soul will believe in it." And what is a novel if not a conviction of our fellow-men's existence strong enough to take upon itself a form of imagined life clearer than reality and whose accumulated verisimilitude of selected episodes puts to shame the pride of documentary history? Providence which saved my MS. from the Congo rapids brought it to the knowledge of a helpful soul far out on the open sea. It would be on my part the greatest ingratitude ever to forget the sallow, sunken face and the deep-set, dark eyes of the young Cambridge man (he was a "passenger for his health" on board the good ship *Torrens* outward bound to Australia) who was the first reader of *Almayer's Folly*—the very first reader I ever had. "Would it bore you very much reading a MS. in a handwriting like mine?" I asked him one evening on a sudden impulse at the end of a longish conversation whose subject was Gibbon's History. Jacques (that was his name) was sitting in my cabin one stormy dog-watch below, after bringing me a book to read from his own traveling store.

"Not at all," he answered, with his courteous intonation and a faint smile. As I pulled a drawer open his suddenly aroused curiosity gave him a watchful expression. I wonder what he expected to see. A poem, maybe. All that's beyond guessing now. He was not a cold, but a calm man, still more subdued by disease—a man of few words and of an unassuming modesty in general intercourse, but with something uncommon in the whole of his person which set him apart from the undistinguished lot of our sixty passengers. His eyes had a thoughtful introspective look. In his attractive, reserved manner, and in a veiled, sympathetic voice, he asked:

"What is this?" "It is a sort of tale," I answered with an effort. "It is not even finished yet. Nevertheless, I would like to know what you think of it." He put the MS. in the breast-pocket of his jacket; I remember perfectly his thin brown fingers folding it lengthwise. "I will read it to-morrow," he remarked, seizing the door-handle, and then, watching the roll of the ship for a propitious moment, he opened the door and was gone. In the moment of his exit I heard the sustained booming of the wind, the swish of the water on the decks of the *Torrens*, and the subdued, as if distant, roar of the rising sea. I noted the growing disquiet in the great restlessness of the ocean, and responded professionally to it with the thought that at eight o'clock, in another half-hour or so at the furthest, the top-gallant sails would have to come off the ship.

Next day, but this time in the first dog-watch, Jacques entered my cabin. He had a thick, woollen muffler round his throat and the MS. was in his hand. He tendered it to me with a steady look but without a word. I took it in silence. He sat down on the couch and still said nothing. I opened and shut the drawer under my desk, on which a filled-up log-slate lay wide open in its wooden frame waiting to be copied neatly into the sort of book I was accustomed to write with care, the ship's log-book. I turned my back squarely on the desk. And even then Jacques never offered a word. "Well, what do you say?" I asked at last. "Is it worth finishing?" This question expressed exactly the whole of my thoughts.

"Distinctly," he answered in his sedate veiled voice, and then coughed a little.

"Were you interested?" I inquired further, almost in a whisper.

"Very much!"

23

In a pause I went on meeting instinctively the heavy rolling of the ship, and Jacques put his feet upon the couch. The curtain of my bed-place swung to and fro as if it were a punkah, the bulkhead lamp circled in its gimbals, and now and then the cabin door rattled slightly in the gusts of wind. It was in latitude 40° south, and nearly in the longitude of Greenwich, as far as I can remember, that these quiet rites of Almayer's and Nina's resurrection were taking place. In the prolonged silence it occurred to me that there was a good deal of retrospective writing in the story as far as it went. Was it intelligible in its action, I asked myself, as if already the story-teller were being born into the body of the seaman. But I heard on deck the whistle of the officer of the watch and remained on the alert to catch the order that was to follow this call to attention. It reached me as a faint, fierce shout to "Square the yards." "Aha!" I thought to myself, "a westerly blow coming on." Then I turned to my very first reader, who, alas! was not to live long enough to know the end of the tale.

"Now let me ask you one more thing: Is the story quite clear to you as it stands?"

He raised his dark, gentle eyes to my face and seemed surprised.

"Yes! Perfectly."

This was all I was to hear from his lips concerning the merits of *Almayer's Folly*. We never spoke together of the book again. A long period of bad weather set in and I had no thoughts left but for my duties, whilst poor Jacques caught a fatal cold and had to keep close in his cabin. When we arrived at Adelaide the first reader of my prose went at once up-country, and died rather suddenly in the end, either in Australia or it may be on the passage while going home through the Suez Canal. I am not sure which it was now, and I do not think I ever heard precisely; though I made inquiries about him from some of our return passengers who, wandering about to "see the country" during the ship's stay in port, had come upon him here and there. At last we sailed, homeward bound, and still not one line was added to the careless scrawl of the many pages which poor Jacques had had the patience to read with the very shadows of Eternity gathered already in the hollows of his kind, steadfast eyes.

The purpose instilled into me by his simple and final "Distinctly" remained dormant, yet alive to wait its opportunity. I dare say I am compelled, unconsciously compelled, now to write volume after volume, as in past years I was compelled to go to sea, voyage after voyage. Leaves must follow upon each other as leagues used to follow in the days gone by, on and on to the appointed end, which, being Truth itself, is One—one for all men and for all occupations.

I do not know which of the two impulses has appeared more mysterious and more wonderful to me. Still, in writing, as in going to sea, I had to wait my opportunity. Let me confess here that I was never one of those wonderful fellows that would go afloat in a wash-tub for the sake of the fun, and if I may pride myself upon my consistency it was ever just the same with my writing. Some men, I have heard, write in railway carriages, and could do it, perhaps, sitting cross-legged on a clothes-line; but I must confess that my sybaritic disposition will not consent to write without something at least resembling a chair. Line by line, rather than page by page, was the growth of *Almayer's Folly*.

And so it happened that I very nearly lost the MS., advanced now to the first words of the ninth chapter, in the Friedrichstrasse railway station (that's in Berlin, you know) on my way to Poland, or more precisely Ukraine. On an early, sleepy morning, changing trains in a hurry, I left my Gladstone bag in a refreshment-room. A worthy and intelligent *Kofferträger* rescued it. Yet in my anxiety I was not thinking of the MS. but of all the other things that were packed in the bag.

In Warsaw, where I spent two days, those wandering pages were never exposed to the light, except once, to candle-light, while the bag lay open on a chair. I was dressing hurriedly to dine at a sporting club. A friend of my childhood (he had been in the Diplomatic Service, but had turned to growing wheat on paternal acres, and we had not seen each other for over twenty years) was sitting on the hotel sofa waiting to carry me off there.

"You might tell me something of your life while you are dressing," he suggested kindly.

I do not think I told him much of my life-story either then or later. The talk of the select little party with which he made me dine was extremely animated and embraced most subjects under heaven, from big-game shooting in Africa to the last poem published in a very modernist review, edited by the very young and patronised by the highest society. But it never touched upon *Almayer's Folly*, and next morning, in uninterrupted obscurity, this inseparable companion went on rolling with me in the south-east direction towards the Government of Kiev.

At that time there was an eight-hours' drive, if not more, from the railway station to the country house which was my destination.

"Dear boy" (these words were always written in English)—so ran the last letter from that house received in London—"Get yourself driven to the only inn in the place, dine as well as you can, and some time in the evening my own confidential servant, factotum and major-domo, a Mr. V.S. (I warn you he is of noble extraction), will present himself before you, reporting the arrival of the small sledge which will take you here on the next day. I send with him my heaviest fur, which I suppose, with such overcoats as you may have with you, will keep you from freezing on the road."

Sure enough, as I was dining, served by a Hebrew waiter, in an enormous barn-like bedroom with a freshly painted floor, the door opened and, in a travelling costume of long

26

boots, big sheep-skin cap and a short coat girt with a leather belt, the Mr. V.S. (of noble extraction), a man of about thirty-five, appeared with an air of perplexity on his open and moustachioed countenance. I got up from the table and greeted him in Polish, with, I hope, the right shade of consideration demanded by his noble blood and his confidential position. His face cleared up in a wonderful way. It appeared that, notwithstanding my uncle's earnest assurances, the good fellow had remained in doubt of our understanding each other. He imagined I would talk to him in some foreign language. I was told that his last words on getting into the sledge to come to meet me shaped an anxious exclamation:

"Well! Well! Here I am going, but God only knows how I am to make myself understood to our master's nephew."

We understood each other very well from the first. He took charge of me as if I were not quite of age. I had a delightful boyish feeling of coming home from school when he muffled me up next morning in an enormous bear-skin travelling-coat and took his seat protectively by my side. The sledge was a very small one and it looked utterly insignificant, almost like a toy behind the four big bays harnessed two and two. We three, counting the coachman, filled it completely. He was a young fellow with clear blue eyes; the high collar of his livery fur coat framed his cheery countenance and stood all round level with the top of his head.

"Now, Joseph," my companion addressed him, "do you think we shall manage to get home before six?" His answer was that we surely would, with God's help, and providing there were no heavy drifts in the long stretch between certain villages whose names came with an extremely familiar sound to my ears. He turned out an excellent coachman with an instinct for keeping the road amongst the snow-covered fields and a natural gift of getting the best out of the horses.

"He is the son of that Joseph that I suppose the Captain

27

remembers. He who used to drive the Captain's late grandmother of holy memory," remarked V.S., busy tucking fur rugs about my feet.

I remembered perfectly the trusty Joseph who used to drive my grandmother. Why! he it was who let me hold the reins for the first time in my life and allowed me to play with the great four-in-hand whip outside the doors of the coach-house.

"What became of him?" I asked. "He is no longer serving, I suppose."

"He served our master," was the reply. "But he died of cholera ten years ago now—that great epidemic we had. And his wife died at the same time—the whole houseful of them, and this is the only boy that was left."

The MS. of *Almayer's Folly* was reposing in the bag under our feet.

I saw again the sun setting on the plains as I saw it in the travels of my childhood. It set, clear and red, dipping into the snow in full view as if it were setting on the sea. It was twenty-three years since I had seen the sun set over that land; and we drove on in the darkness which fell swiftly upon the livid expanse of snows till, out of the waste of a white earth joining a bestarred sky, surged up black shapes, the clumps of trees about a village of the Ukrainian plain. A cottage or two glided by, a low interminable wall and then, glimmering and winking through a screen of fir-trees, the lights of the master's house.

That very evening the wandering MS. of *Almayer's Folly* was unpacked and unostentatiously laid on the writing-table in my room, the guest-room which had been, I was informed in an affectedly careless tone, awaiting me for some fifteen years or so. It attracted no attention from the affectionate presence hovering round the son of the favourite sister.

"You won't have many hours to yourself while you are staying with me, brother," he said—this form of address borrowed from the speech of our peasants being the usual expression of the highest good humour in a moment of affectionate elation. "I shall always be coming in for a chat.",

As a matter of fact we had the whole house to chat in and were everlastingly intruding upon each other. I invaded the retirement of his study, where the principal feature was a colossal silver inkstand presented to him on his fiftieth year by a subscription of all his wards then living. He had been guardian of many orphans of land-owning families from the three southern provinces—ever since the year 1860. Some of them had been my school-fellows and playmates, but not one of them, girls or boys, that I know of, has ever written a novel. One or two were older than myself—considerably older, too. One of them, a visitor I remember in my early years, was the man who first put me on horseback, and his four-horse bachelor turn-out, his perfect horsemanship and general skill in manly exercises was one of my earliest admirations. I seem to remember my mother looking on from a colonnade in front of the dining-room window as I was lifted upon the pony, held, for all I know, by the very Joseph—the groom attached specially to my grandmother's service—who died of cholera. It was certainly a young man in a dark blue, tail-less coat and huge Cossack trousers, that being the livery of the men about the stables. It must have been in 1864, but reckoning by another mode of calculating time, it was certainly in the year in which my mother obtained permission to travel south and visit her family, from the exile into which she had followed my father. For that, too, she had had to ask permission, and I know that one of the conditions of that favour was that she should be treated exactly as a condemned exile herself. Yet a couple of years later, in memory of her eldest brother who had served in the Guards and dying early left hosts of friends and a loved memory in the great world of St. Petersburg, some influential personages procured for her this permission—it was officially called the

"Highest Grace"—of a three months' leave from exile.

This is also the year in which I first begin to remember my mother with more distinctness than a mere loving, wide-browed, silent, protecting presence, whose eyes had a sort of commanding sweetness; and I also remember the great gathering of all the relations from near and far, and the grey heads of the family friends paying her the homage of respect and love in the house of her favourite brother who, a few years later, was to take the place for me of both my parents.

I did not understand the tragic significance of it all at the time, though indeed I remember that doctors also came. There were no signs of invalidism about her—but I think that already they had pronounced her doom unless perhaps the change to a southern climate could re-establish her declining strength. For me it seems the very happiest period of my existence. There was my cousin, a delightful, quick-tempered little girl, some months younger than myself, whose life, lovingly watched over, as if she were a royal princess, came to an end with her fifteenth year. There were other children too, many of whom are dead now, and not a few whose very names I have forgotten. Over all this hung the oppressive shadow of the great Russian Empire—the shadow lowering with the darkness of a new-born national hatred fostered by the Moscow school of journalists against the Poles after the ill-omened rising of 1863.

This is a far cry back from the MS. of *Almayer's Folly* but the public record of these formative impressions is not the whim of an uneasy egotism. These, too, are things human, already distant in their appeal. It is meet that something more should be left for the novelist's children than the colours and figures of his own hard-won creation. That which in their grown-up years may appear to the world about them as the most enigmatic side of their natures and perhaps must remain for ever obscure even to themselves, will be their unconscious response to the

30

still voice of that inexorable past from which his work of fiction and their personalities are remotely derived.

Only in men's imagination does every truth find an effective and undeniable existence. Imagination, not invention, is the supreme master of art as of life. An imaginative and exact rendering of authentic memories may serve worthily that spirit of piety towards all things human which sanctions the conceptions of a writer of tales, and the emotions of the man reviewing his own experience.

II

A S I have said, I was unpacking my luggage after a journey from London into Ukraine. The M.S. of *Almayer's Folly*—my companion already for some three years or more, and then in the ninth chapter of its age— was deposited unostentatiously on the writing-table placed between two windows. It didn't occur to me to put it away in the drawer the table was fitted with, but my eye was attracted by the good form of the same drawer's brass handles. Two candelabra, with four candles each, lighted up festally the room which had waited so many years for the wandering nephew. The blinds were down.

Within five hundred yards of the chair on which I sat stood the first peasant hut of the village—part of my maternal grandfather's estate, the only part remaining in the possession of a member of the family; and beyond the village in the limitless blackness of a winter's night there lay the great unfenced fields—not a flat and severe plain, but a kindly, bread-giving land of low, rounded ridges, all white now, with the black patches of timber nestling in the hollows. The road by which I had come ran through a village with a turn just outside the gates closing the short drive. Somebody was abroad on the deep snow-track; a quick tinkle of bells stole gradually into the stillness of the room like a tuneful whisper.

My unpacking had been watched over by the servant who had come to help me, and, for the most part, had been standing attentive but unnecessary at the door of the room. I did not want him in the least, but I did not like to tell him to go away. He was a young fellow, certainly more than ten years younger than myself; I had not been—I won't say in that place but within sixty miles of it, ever since the year '67; yet his guileless physiognomy of the open peasant type seemed strangely familiar. It was quite possible that he might have been a descendant, a son or even a grandson, of the servants whose friendly faces had been familiar to me in my early childhood. As a matter of fact he had no such claim on my consideration. He was the product of some village near by and was there on his promotion, having learned the service in one or two houses as pantry-boy. I know this because I asked the worthy V——next day. I might well have spared the question. I discovered before long that all the faces about the house and all the faces in the village: the grave faces with long moustaches of the heads of families, the downy faces of the young men, the faces of the little fair-haired children, the handsome, tanned, wide-browed faces of the mothers seen at the doors of the huts, were as familiar to me as though I had known them all from childhood, and my childhood were a matter of the day before yesterday.

The tinkle of the traveller's bells, after growing louder, had faded away quickly, and the tumult of barking dogs in the village had calmed down at last. My uncle, lounging in the corner of a small couch, smoked his long Turkish *chibouk* in silence.

"This is an extremely nice writing-table you have got for my room," I remarked.

"It is really your property," he said, keeping his eyes on me, with an interested and wistful expression, as he had done ever since I entered the house. "Forty years ago your mother used to write at this very table. In our house in Oratow it stood in the little sitting-room which, by a tacit agreement, was given up to the girls—I mean to your mother and her sister who died so young. It was a present to them jointly from our uncle Nicholas B. when your mother was seventeen and your aunt two years younger. She was a very dear, delightful girl, that aunt of yours, of whom I suppose you know nothing more than the name. She did not shine so much by personal beauty and a cultivated mind, in which your mother was far superior. It was her good sense, the admirable sweetness of her nature, her exceptional facility and ease in daily relations that endeared her to everybody. Her death was a terrible grief and a serious moral loss for us all. Had she lived she would have brought the greatest blessings to the house it would have been her lot to enter, as wife, mother and mistress of a household. She would have created round herself an atmosphere of peace and content which only those who can love unselfishly are able to evoke. Your mother—of far greater beauty, exceptionally distinguished in person, manner and intellect—had a less easy disposition. Being more brilliantly gifted, she also expected more from life. At that trying time, especially, we were greatly concerned about her state. Suffering in her health from the shock of her father's death (she was alone in the house with him when he died suddenly), she was torn by the inward struggle between her love for the man whom she was to marry in the end and her knowledge of her dead father's declared objection to that match. Unable to bring herself to disregard that cherished memory and that judgment she had always respected and trusted, and, on the other hand, feeling the imposssibility to resist a sentiment so deep and so true, she could not have been expected to preserve her mental and moral balance. At war with herself, she could not give to others that feeling of peace which was not her own. It was only later, when united at last with the man of her choice, that she developed those uncommon gifts of mind and heart which compelled the respect and admiration even of our foes. Meeting with calm fortitude the cruel trials of a life reflecting all the national and social misfortunes of the community, she realised the highest conceptions of duty as a wife, a mother and a patriot, sharing the exile of her husband and representing nobly the ideal of Polish womanhood. Our Uncle Nicholas was not a man very accessible to feelings of affection. Apart from his worship for Napoleon the Great, he loved really, I believe, only three people in the world: his mother—your great-grandmother, whom you have seen but cannot possibly remember; his brother, our father, in whose house he lived for so many years; and of all of us, his nephews and nieces grown up around him, your mother alone. The modest, lovable qualities of the youngest sister he did not seem able to see. It was I who felt most profoundly this unexpected stroke of death falling upon the family less than a year after I had become its head. It was terribly unexpected. Driving home one wintry afternoon to keep me company in our empty house, where I had to remain permanently administering the estate and attending to the complicated affairs—the girls took it in turn week and week about—driving, as I said, from the house of the Countess Tekla Potocka, where our invalid mother was staying then to be near a doctor, they lost the road and got stuck in a snowdrift. She was alone with the coachman and old Valery, the personal servant of our late father. Impatient of delay while they were trying to dig themselves out, she jumped out of the sledge and went to look for the road herself. All this happened in '51, not ten miles from the house in which we are sitting now. The road was soon found, but snow had begun to fall thickly again, and they were four more hours getting home. Both the men took off their sheepskin-lined great-coats and used all their own rugs to wrap her up against the cold, notwithstanding her protests, positive orders and even

36

struggles, as Valery afterwards related to me. 'How could I,' he remonstrated with her, 'go to meet the blessed soul of my late master if I let any harm come to you while there's a spark of life left in my body?' When they reached home, at last, the poor old man was stiff and speechless from exposure, and the coachman was in not much better plight, though he had the strength to drive round to the stables himself. To my reproaches for venturing out at all in such weather, she answered characteristically that she could not bear the thought of abandoning me to my cheerless solitude. It is incomprehensible how it was that she was allowed to start. I suppose it had to be! She made light of the cough which came on next day, but shortly afterwards inflammation of the lungs set in, and in three weeks she was no more! She was the first to be taken away of the young generation under my care. Behold the vanity of all hopes and fears! I was the most frail at birth of all the children. For years I remained so delicate that my parents had but little hope of bringing me up; I have outlived my wife and daughter, too—and from all those who have had some knowledge at least of these old times, you alone are left. It has been my lot to lay in an early grave many honest hearts, many brilliant promises, many hopes full of life.''

He got up brusquely, sighed, and left me, saying: ''We will dine in half an hour.'' Without moving, I listened to his quick steps resounding on the waxed floor of the next room, traversing the ante-room lined with bookshelves, where he paused to put his *chibouk* in the pipe-stand before passing into the drawing-room (these were all *en suite*), where he became inaudible on the thick carpet. But I heard the door of his study-bedroom close. He was then sixty-two years old and had been for a quarter of a century the wisest, the firmest, the most indulgent of guardians, extending over me a paternal care and affection, a moral support which I seemed to feel always near me in the most distant parts of the earth.

As to Mr. Nicholas B., sub-lieutenant of 1808, lieutenant of 1813 in the French Army, and for a short time *Officier d'Ordonnance* of Marshal Marmont; afterwards Captain in the 2nd Regiment of Mounted Rifles in the Polish Army—such as it existed up to 1830 in the reduced kingdom established by the Congress of Vienna—I must say that from all that more distant past, known to me traditionally and a little *de visu*, and called out by the words of the man just gone away, he remains the most incomplete figure. It is obvious that I must have seen him in '64, for it is certain that he would not have missed the opportunity of seeing my mother for what he must have known would be the last time. From my early boyhood to this day, if I try to call up his image, a sort of mist rises before my eyes, a mist in which I perceive vaguely only a neatly brushed head of white hair (which is exceptional in the case of the B. family, where it is the rule for the men to go bald in a becoming manner, before thirty) and a thin, curved, dignified nose, a feature in strict accordance with the physical tradition of the B. family. But it is not by these fragmentary remains of a perishable mortality that he lives in my memory. I knew, at a very early age, that my grand-uncle Nicholas B. was a Knight of the Legion of Honour and that he had also the Polish Cross for valour, *Virtuti Militari*. The knowledge of these glorious facts inspired in me an admiring veneration; yet it is not that sentiment, strong as it was, which resumes for me the force and the significance of his personality. It is overborne by another and complex impression of awe, compassion and horror. Mr. Nicholas B. remains for me the unfortunate and miserable (but heroic) being who once upon a time had eaten a dog.

It is a good forty years since I heard the tale, and the effect has not worn off yet. I believe this is the very first, say, realistic, story I heard in my life; but all the same, I don't know why I should have been so frightfully impressed. Of course I know what our village dogs look

like—but still ... No! At this very day, recalling the
horror and compassion of my childhood, I ask myself
whether I am right in disclosing to a cold and fastidious
world that awful episode in the family history. I ask
myself—is it right?—especially as the B. family had always been honourably known in a wide country-side for
the delicacy of their tastes in the matter of eating and
drinking. But upon the whole, and considering that this
gastronomical degradation overtaking a gallant young officer lies really at the door of the Great Napoleon, I think
that to cover it up by silence would be an exaggeration of
literary restraint. Let the truth stand here. The responsibility rests with the Man of St. Helena in view of his
deplorable levity in the conduct of the Russian campaign.
It was during the memorable retreat from Moscow that
Mr. Nicholas B., in company of two brother officers—as
to whose morality and natural refinement I know
nothing—bagged a dog on the outskirts of a village and
subsequently devoured him. As far as I can remember, the
weapon used was a cavalry sabre, and the issue of the
sporting episode was rather more of a matter of life and
death than if it had been an encounter with a tiger. A
picket of Cossacks was sleeping in that village lost in the
depths of the great Lithuanian forest. The three sports-
men had observed them from a hiding-place making
themselves very much at home amongst the huts just
before the early winter darkness set in at four o'clock.
They had observed them with disgust and perhaps with
despair. Late in the night the rash counsels of hunger
overcame the dictates of prudence. Crawling through the
snow, they crept up to the fence of dry branches which
generally encloses a village in that part of Lithuania. What
they expected to get, and in what manner, and whether
this expectation was worth the risk, goodness only
knows. However, these Cossack parties, in most cases
wandering without an officer, were known to guard themselves badly and often not at all. In addition, the village

lying at a great distance from the line of French retreat, they could not suspect the presence of stragglers from the Grand Army. The three officers had strayed away in a blizzard from the main column and had been lost for days in the woods, which explains sufficiently the terrible straits to which they were reduced. Their plan was to try and attract the attention of the peasants in that one of the huts which was nearest to the enclosure; but as they were preparing to venture into the very jaws of the lion, so to speak, a dog (it is mighty strange that there was but one), a creature quite as formidable under the circumstances as a lion, began to bark on the other side of the fence. . . .

At this stage of the narrative, which I heard many times (by request) from the lips of Captain Nicholas B.'s sister-in-law, my grandmother, I used to tremble with excitement.

The dog barked. And if he had done no more than bark, three officers of the Great Napoleon's army would have perished honourably on the points of Cossacks' lances, or perhaps escaping the chase, would have died decently of starvation. But before they had time to think of running away, that fatal and revolting dog, being carried away by the excess of his zeal, dashed out through a gap in the fence. He dashed out and died. His head, I understand, was severed at one blow from his body. I understand also that, later on, within the gloomy solitudes of the snow-laden woods, when in a sheltering hollow a fire had been lit by the party, the condition of the quarry was discovered to be distinctly unsatisfactory. It was not thin—on the contrary, it seemed unhealthily obese; its skin showed bare patches of an unpleasant character. However, they had not killed that dog for the sake of the pelt. He was large. . . . He was eaten. . . . The rest is silence. . . . A silence in which a small boy shudders and says firmly:

"I could not have eaten that dog."

And his grandmother remarks with a smile:

"Perhaps you don't know what it is to be hungry."

I have learned something of it since. Not that I have been reduced to eat dog. I have fed on the emblematical animal, which, in the language of the volatile Gauls, is called *la vache enragée*; I have lived on ancient salt junk, I know the taste of shark, of trepang, of snake, of nondescript dishes containing things without a name—but of the Lithuanian village dog, never! I wish it to be distinctly understood that it is not I, but my grand-uncle Nicholas, of the Polish landed gentry, *Chevalier de la Légion d'Honneur*, etc., etc., who, in his young days, had eaten the Lithuanian dog.

I wish he had not. The childish horror of the deed clings absurdly to the grizzled man. I am perfectly helpless against it. Still, if he really had to, let us charitably remember that he had eaten him on active service, while bearing up bravely against the greatest military disaster of modern history, and, in a manner, for the sake of his country. Her had eaten him to appease his hunger, no doubt, but also for the sake of an unappeasable and patriotic desire, in the glow of a great faith that lives still, and in the pursuit of a great illusion kindled like a false beacon by a great many to lead astray the effort of a brave nation.

Pro patria!

Looked at in that light it appears a sweet and decorous meal.

And looked at in the same light, my own diet of *la vache enragée* appears a fatuous and extravagant form of self-indulgence; for why should I, the son of a land which such men as these have turned up with their ploughshares and bedewed with their blood, undertake the pursuit of fantastic meals of salt junk and hard tack upon the wide seas? On the kindest view it seems an unanswerable question. Alas! I have the conviction that there are men of unstained rectitude who are ready to murmur scornfully the word desertion. Thus the taste of innocent adventure may be made bitter to the palate. The part of the inexplicable should be allowed for in appraising the conduct of men in a world where no explanation is final. No charge of faithlessness ought to be uttered lightly. The appearances of this perishable life are deceptive like everything that falls under the judgment of our imperfect senses. The inner voice may remain true enough in its secret counsel. The fidelity to a special tradition may last through the events of an unrelated existence, following faithfully, too, the traced way of an inexplicable impulse.

It would take too long to explain the intimate alliance of contradictions in human nature which makes love itself wear at times the desperate shape of betrayal. And perhaps there is no possible explanation. Indulgence—as somebody said—is the most intelligent of all the virtues. I venture to think that it is one of the least common, if not the most uncommon of all. I would not imply by this that men are foolish—or even most men. Far from it. The barber and the priest, backed by the whole opinion of the village, condemned justly the conduct of the ingenious hidalgo who, sallying forth from his native place, broke the head of the muleteer, put to death a flock of inoffensive sheep, and went through very doleful experiences in a certain stable. God forbid that an unworthy churl should escape merited censure by hanging on to the stirrup-leather of the sublime *caballero*. His was a very noble, a very unselfish fantasy, fit for nothing except to raise the envy of baser mortals. But there is more than one aspect to the charm of that exalted and dangerous figure. He, too, had his frailties. After reading so many romances he desired naïvely to escape with his very body from the intolerable reality of things. He wished to meet eye to eye the valorous giant Brandabarbaran, Lord of Arabia, whose armour is made of the skin of a dragon, and whose shield, strapped to his arm, is the gate of a fortified city. O amiable and natural weakness! O blessed simplicity of a gentle heart without guile! Who would not succumb to such a consoling temptation? Nevertheless it was a form of

42

self-indulgence, and the ingenious hidalgo of La Mancha was not a good citizen. The priest and the barber were not unreasonable in their strictures. Without going so far as the old King Louis-Philippe, who used to say in his exile, "The people are never in fault"—one may admit that there must be some righteousness in the assent of a whole village. Mad! Mad! He who kept in pious meditation the ritual vigil-of-arms by the well of an inn and knelt reverently to be knighted at daybreak by the fat, sly rogue of a landlord, has come very near perfection. He rides forth, his head encircled by a halo—the patron saint of all lives spoiled or saved by the irresistible grace of imagination. But he was not a good citizen.

Perhaps that and nothing else was meant by the well-remembered exclamation of my tutor.

It was in the jolly year 1873, the very last year in which I have had a jolly holiday. There have been idle years afterwards, jolly enough in a way and not altogether without their lesson, but this year of which I speak was the year of my last schoolboy holiday. There are other reasons why I should remember that year, but they are too long to state formally in this place. Moreover they have nothing to do with that holiday. What has to do with the holiday is that before the day on which the remark was made we had seen Vienna, the Upper Danube, Munich, the Falls of the Rhine, the Lake of Constance—in fact it was a memorable holiday of travel. Of late we had been tramping slowly up the Valley of the Reuss. It was a delightful time. It was much more like a stroll than a tramp. Landing from a Lake of Lucerne steamer in Fluellen, we found ourselves at the end of the second day, with the dusk overtaking our leisurely footsteps, a little way beyond Hospenthal. This is not the day on which the remark was made: in the shadows of the deep valley and with the habitations of men left some way behind, our thoughts ran not upon the ethics of conduct but upon the simpler human problem of shelter and food. There did not seem anything of the kind in sight, and we were thinking of turning back when suddenly at a bend of the road we came upon a building, ghostly in the twilight.

At that time the work on the St. Gothard Tunnel was going on, and that magnificent enterprise of burrowing was directly responsible for the unexpected building standing all alone upon the very roots of the mountains. It was long, though not big at all; it was low; it was built of boards, without ornamentation, in barrack hut style, with the white window-frames quite flush with the yellow face of its plain front. And yet it was an hotel; it had even a name which I have forgotten. But there was no gold-laced doorkeeper at its humble door. A plain but vigorous servant-girl answered our inquiries, then a man and woman who owned the place appeared. It was clear that no travellers were expected, or perhaps even desired, in this strange hostelry, which in its severe style resembled the house which surmounts the unseaworthy-looking hulls of the toy Noah's Arks, the universal possession of European childhood. However, its roof was not hinged and it was not full to the brim of slab-sided and painted animals of wood. Even the live tourist animal was nowhere in evidence. We had something to eat in a long, narrow room at one end of a long, narrow table, which, to my tired perception and to my sleepy eyes, seemed as if it would tilt up like a see-saw plank, since there was no one at the other end to balance it against our two dusty and travel-stained figures. Then we hastened upstairs to bed in a room smelling of pine planks, and I was fast asleep before my head touched the pillow.

In the morning my tutor (he was a student of the Cracow University) woke me up early, and as we were dressing remarked: "There seems to be a lot of people staying in this hotel. I have heard a noise of talking up till eleven o'clock." This statement surprised me; I had heard no noise whatever, having slept like a top.

We went downstairs into the long and narrow dining

room with its long and narrow table. There were two rows of plates on it. At one of the many uncurtained windows stood a tall, bony man with a bald head set off by a bunch of black hair above each ear and with a long black beard. He glanced up from the paper he was reading and seemed genuinely astonished at our intrusion. By and by more men came in. Not one of them looked like a tourist. Not a single woman appeared. These men seemed to know each other with some intimacy, but I cannot say they were a very talkative lot. The bald-headed man sat down gravely at the head of the table. It all had the air of a family party. By and by, from one of the vigorous servant-girls in national costume, we discovered that the place was really a boarding-house for some English engineers engaged at the works of the St. Gothard Tunnel; and I could listen my fill to the sounds of the English language as far as it is used at a breakfast-table by men who do not believe in wasting many words on the mere amenities of life.

This was my first contact with British mankind apart from the tourist kind seen in the hotels of Zurich and Lucerne—the kind which has no real existence in a workaday world. I know now that the bald-headed man spoke with a strong Scotch accent. I have met many of his kind since, both ashore and afloat. The second engineer of the steamer *Mavis*, for instance, ought to have been his twin brother. I cannot help thinking that he really was, though for some reason of his own he assured me that he never had a twin brother. Anyway, the deliberate, bald-headed Scot with the coal-black beard appeared to my boyish eyes a very romantic and mysterious person.

We slipped out unnoticed. Our mapped-out route led over the Furca Pass towards the Rhône Glacier, with the further intention of following down the trend of the Häsli Valley. The sun was already declining when we found ourselves on the top of the pass, and the remark alluded to was presently uttered.

45

We sat down by the side of the road to continue the argument begun half a mile or so before. I am certain it was an argument because I remember perfectly how my tutor argued and how without the power of reply I listened with my eyes fixed obstinately on the ground. A stir on the road made me look up—and then I saw my unforgettable Englishman. There are acquaintances of later years, familiars, shipmates, whom I remember less clearly. He marched rapidly towards the east (attended by a hang-dog Swiss guide) with the mien of an ardent and fearless traveller. He was clad in a knickerbocker suit, but as at the same time he wore short socks under his laced boots, for reasons which, whether hygienic or conscientious, were surely imaginative, his calves exposed to the public gaze and to the tonic air of high altitudes, dazzled the beholder by the splendour of their marble-like condition and their rich tone of young ivory. He was the leader of a small caravan. The light of a headlong, exalted satisfaction with the world of men and the scenery of mountains illumined his clean-cut, very red face, his short, silver-white whiskers, his innocently eager and triumphant eyes. In passing he cast a glance of kindly curiosity and a friendly gleam of big, sound, shiny teeth towards the man and the boy sitting like dusty tramps by the roadside, with a modest knapsack lying at their feet. His white calves twinkled sturdily, the uncouth Swiss guide with a surly mouth stalked like an unwilling bear at his elbow; a small train of three mules followed in single file the lead of this inspiring enthusiast. Two ladies rode past one behind the other, but from the way they sat I only saw their calm, uniform backs, and the long ends of blue veils hanging behind far down over their identical hat-brims. His two daughters, surely. An industrious luggage-mule, with unstarched ears and guarded by a slouching, sallow driver, brought up the rear. My tutor, after pausing for a look and a faint smile, resumed his earnest argument.

I tell you it was a memorable year! One does not meet such an Englishman twice in a lifetime. Was he in the mystic ordering of common events the ambassador of my future, sent out to turn the scale at a critical moment on the top of an Alpine pass, with the peaks of the Bernese Oberland for mute and solemn witnesses? His glance, his smile, the unextinguishable and comic ardour of his striving-forward appearance helped me to pull myself together. It must be stated that on that day and in the exhilarating atmosphere of that elevated spot I had been feeling utterly crushed. It was the year in which I had first spoken aloud of my desire to go to sea. At first, like those sounds that, ranging outside the scale to which men's ears are attuned, remain inaudible to our sense of hearing, this declaration passed unperceived. It was as if it had not been. Later on, by trying various tones, I managed to arouse here and there a surprised momentary attention—the "What was that funny noise?" sort of inquiry. Later on it was—"Did you hear what that boy said? What an extraordinary outbreak!" Presently a wave of scandalised astonishment (it could not have been greater if I had announced the intention of entering a Carthusian monastery) ebbing out of the educational and academical town of Cracow spread itself over several provinces. It spread itself shallow but far-reaching. It stirred up a mass of remonstrance, indignation, pitying wonder, bitter irony and downright chaff. I could hardly breathe under its weight, and certainly had no words for an answer. People wondered what Mr. T.B. would do now with his worrying nephew and, I dare say, hoped kindly that he would make short work of my nonsense.

What he did was to come all the way down from Ukraine to have it out with me and to judge by himself, unprejudiced, impartial and just, taking his stand on the ground of wisdom and affection. As far as is possible for a boy whose power of expression is still unformed, I opened the secret of my thoughts to him and he in return allowed

47

me to glimpse into his mind and heart; the first glimpse of an inexhaustible and noble treasure of clear thought and warm feeling, which through life was to be mine to draw upon with a never-deceived love and confidence. Practically, after several exhaustive conversations, he concluded that he would not have me later on reproach him for having spoiled my life by an unconditional opposition. But I must take time for serious reflection. And I must not only think of myself but of others; weigh the claims of affection and conscience against my own sincerity of purpose. "Think well what it all means in the larger issues, my boy," he exhorted me finally with special friendliness. "And meantime try to get the best place you can at the yearly examinations."

The scholastic year came to an end. I took a fairly good place at the exams, which for me (for certain reasons) happened to be a more difficult task than for other boys. In that respect I could enter with a good conscience upon that holiday which was like a long visit *pour prendre congé* of the mainland of old Europe I was to see so little for the next four-and-twenty years. Such, however, was not the avowed purpose of that tour. It was rather, I suspect, planned in order to distract and occupy my thoughts in other directions. Nothing had been said for months of my going to sea. But my attachment to my young tutor and his influence over me were so well known that he must have received a confidential mission to talk me out of my romantic folly. It was an excellently appropriate arrangement, as neither he nor I had ever had a single glimpse of the sea in our lives. That was to come by and by for both of us in Venice, from the outer shore of Lido. Meantime he had taken his mission to heart so well that I began to feel crushed before we reached Zurich. He argued in railway trains, in lake steamboats, he had argued away for me the obligatory sunrise on the Rigi, by Jove! Of his devotion to his unworthy pupil there can be no doubt. He had proved it already by two years of un-

48

remitting and arduous care. I could not hate him. But he had been crushing me slowly, and when he started to argue on the top of the Furca Pass he was perhaps nearer a success than either he or I imagined. I listened to him in despairing silence, feeling that ghostly, unrealised and desired sea of my dreams escape from the unnerved grip of my will.

The enthusiastic old Englishman had passed—and the argument went on. What reward could I expect from such a life at the end of my years, either in ambition, honour or conscience? An unanswerable question. But I felt no longer crushed. Then our eyes met and a genuine emotion was visible in his as well as in mine. The end came all at once. He picked up the knapsack suddenly and got on to his feet.

"You are an incorrigible, hopeless Don Quixote. That's what you are."

I was surprised. I was only fifteen and did not know what he meant exactly. But I felt vaguely flattered at the name of the immortal knight turning up in connection with my own folly, as some people would call it to my face. Alas! I don't think there was anything to be proud of. Mine was not the stuff the protectors of forlorn damsels, the redressers of this world's wrongs are made of; and my tutor was the man to know that best. Therein, in his indignation, he was superior to the barber and the priest when he flung at me an honoured name like a reproach.

I walked behind him for full five minutes; then without looking back he stopped. The shadows of distant peaks were lengthening over the Furca Pass. When I came up to him he turned to me and in full view of the Finster-Aarhorn, with his band of giant brothers rearing their monstrous heads against a brilliant sky, put his hand on my shoulder affectionately.

"Well! That's enough. We will have no more of it."

And indeed there was no more question of my mysterious vocation between us. There was to be no more question of it at all, nowhere or with any one. We began the descent of the Furca Pass conversing merrily. Eleven years later, month for month, I stood on Tower Hill on the steps of the St. Katherine's Dockhouse, a master in the British Merchant Service. But the man who put his hand on my shoulder at the top of the Furca Pass was no longer living.

That very year of our travels he took his degree of the Philosophical Faculty—and only then his true vocation declared itself. Obedient to the call, he entered at once upon the four-year course of the Medical Schools. A day came when, on the deck of a ship moored in Calcutta, I opened a letter telling me of the end of an enviable existence. He had made for himself a practice in some obscure little town of Austrian Galicia. And the letter went on to tell me how all the bereaved people of the district, Christians and Jews alike, had mobbed the good doctor's coffin with sobs and lamentations at the very gate of the cemetery.

How short his years and how clear his vision! What greater reward in ambition, honour and conscience could he have hoped to win for himself when, on top of the Furca Pass, he bade me look well to the end of my opening life.

III

THE devouring in a dismal forest of a luckless Lithuanian dog by my grand-uncle Nicholas B. in company of two other military and famished scarecrows, symbolised, to my childish imagination, the whole horror of the retreat from Moscow and the immorality of a conqueror's ambition. An extreme distaste for that objectionable episode has tinged the views I hold as to the character and achievements of Napoleon the Great. I need not say that these are unfavourable. It was morally reprehensible for that great captain to induce a simple-minded Polish gentleman to eat dog by raising in his breast a false hope of national independence. It had been the fate of that credulous nation to starve for upwards of a hundred years on a diet of false hopes and—well—dog. It is, when one thinks of it, a singularly poisonous regimen. Some pride in the national constitution which has survived a long course of such dishes is really excusable. But enough of generalising. Returning to particulars, Mr. Nicholas B. confided to his sister-in-law (my grandmother) in his misanthropically laconic manner that this supper in the woods had been nearly "the death of him." This is not surprising. What surprises me is that the story was ever heard of; for grand-uncle Nicholas differed in this from the generality of military men of Napoleon's time (and perhaps of all time), that he did not like to talk of his campaigns, which began at Friedland and ended somewhere in the neighbourhood of Bar-le-Duc. His admiration of the great Emperor was unreserved in everything but expression. Like the religion of earnest men, it was too profound a sentiment to be displayed before a world of little faith. Apart from that he seemed as completely devoid of military anecdotes as though he had hardly ever seen a soldier in his life. Proud of his decorations, earned before he was twenty-five, he refused to wear the ribbons at the buttonhole in the manner practised to this day in Europe and even was unwilling to display the insignia on festive occasions, as though he wished to conceal them in the fear of appearing boastful. "It is enough that I have them," he used to mutter. In the course of thirty years they were seen on his breast only twice—at an auspicious marriage in the family and at the funeral of an old friend. That the wedding which was thus honoured was not the wedding of my mother, I learned only late in life, too late to bear a grudge against Mr. Nicholas B., who made amends at my birth by a long letter of congratulation containing the following prophecy: "He will see better times." Even in his embittered heart there lived hope. But he was not a true prophet.

He was a man of strange contradictions. Living for many years in his brother's house, the home of many children, a house full of life, of animation, noisy with a constant coming and going of many guests, he kept his habits of solitude and silence. Considered as obstinately secretive in all his purposes, he was in reality the victim of a most painful irresolution in all matters of civil life. Under his taciturn, phlegmatic behaviour was hidden a faculty of short-lived, passionate anger. I suspect he had no talent for narrative; but it seemed to afford him sombre satisfaction to declare that he was the last man to ride over the bridge of the river Elster after the battle of Leipsic. Lest some construction favourable to his valour should be put on the fact, he condescended to explain how it came to pass. It seems that shortly after the retreat began he was sent back to the town where some divisions of the French Army (and amongst them the Polish corps of Prince Joseph Poniatowski), jammed hopelessly in the streets, were being simply exterminated by the troops of the Allied Powers. When asked what it was like in there, Mr. Nicholas B. muttered the only word "Shambles." Having delivered this message to the Prince he hastened away at once to render an account of his mission to the superior who had sent him. By that time the advance of the enemy had enveloped the town, and he was shot at from houses and chased all the way to the river bank by a disorderly mob of Austrian Dragoons and Prussian Hussars. The bridge had been mined early in the morning and his opinion was that the sight of the horsemen converging from many sides in the pursuit of his person alarmed the officer in command of the sappers and caused the premature firing of the charges. He had not gone more than 200 yards on the other side when he heard the sound of the fatal explosions. Mr. Nicholas B. concluded his bald narrative with the word "Imbecile," uttered with the utmost deliberation. It testified to his indignation at the loss of so many thousands of lives. But his phlegmatic physiognomy lighted up when he spoke of his only wound, with something resembling satisfaction. You will see that there was some reason for it when you learn that he was wounded in the heel. "Like his Majesty the Emperor Napoleon himself," he reminded his hearers with assumed indifference. There can be no doubt that the indifference was assumed if one thinks what a very distinguished sort of wound it was. In all the history of warfare there are, I believe, only three warriors publicly known to have been wounded in the heel—Achilles and Napoleon—demigods indeed—to whom the familial piety of an unworthy descendant adds the name of the simple mortal, Nicholas B.

The Hundred Days found Mr. Nicholas B. staying with a distant relative of ours, owner of a small estate in Galicia. How he got there across the breadth of an armed Europe and after what adventures I am afraid will never be known now. All his papers were destroyed shortly before his death; but if there was amongst them, as he affirmed, a concise record of his life, then I am pretty sure it did not take up more than a half-sheet of foolscap or so. This relative of ours happened to be an Austrian officer, who had left the service after the battle of Austerlitz. Unlike Mr. Nicholas B., who concealed his decorations, he liked to display his honourable discharge in which he was mentioned as *unschreckbar* (fearless) before the enemy. No conjunction could seem more unpromising, yet it stands in the family tradition that these two got on very well together in their rural solitude.

When asked whether he had not been sorely tempted during the Hundred Days to make his way again to France and join the service of his beloved Emperor, Mr. Nicholas B. used to mutter: "No money. No horse. Too far to walk."

The fall of Napoleon and the ruin of national hopes affected adversely the character of Mr. Nicholas B. He shrank from returning to his province. But for that there was also another reason. Mr. Nicholas B. and his brother—my maternal grandfather—had lost their father early, while they were quite young children. Their mother, young still and left very well off, married again a man of great charm and an amiable disposition but without a penny. He turned out an affectionate and careful stepfather; it was unfortunate though that while directing the boys' education and forming their character by wise counsel he did his best to get hold of the fortune by buying and selling land in his own name and investing capital in such a manner as to cover up the traces of the real ownership. It seems that such practices can be successful if one is charming enough to dazzle one's own

wife permanently and brave enough to defy the vain terrors of public opinion. The critical time came when the
elder of the boys on attaining his majority in the year
1811 asked for the accounts and some part at least of the
inheritance to begin life upon. It was then that the stepfather declared with calm finality that there were no accounts to render and no property to inherit. The whole
fortune was his very own. He was very good-natured
about the young man's misapprehension of the true state
of affairs, but of course felt obliged to maintain his position firmly. Old friends came and went busily, voluntary
mediators appeared travelling on most horrible roads from
the most distant corners of the three provinces; and the
Marshal of the Nobility (*ex-officio* guardian of all well-
born orphans) called a meeting of landowners to "as-
certain in a friendly way how the misunderstanding
between X and his stepsons had arisen and devise proper
measures to remove the same." A deputation to that effect visited X, who treated them to excellent wines, but
absolutely refused his ear to their remonstrances. As to
the proposals for arbitration he simply laughed at them;
yet the whole province must have been aware that fourteen years before, when he married the widow, all his
visible fortune consisted (apart from his social qualities)
in a smart four-horse turn-out with two servants, with
whom he went about visiting from house to house; and as
to any funds he might have possessed at that time their
existence could only be inferred from the fact that he was
very punctual in settling his modest losses at cards. But
by the magic power of stubborn and constant assertion,
there were found presently, here and there, people who
mumbled that surely "there must be something in it."
However, on his next name-day (which he used to cele-
brate by a great three-days' shooting-party), of all the invited crowd only two guests turned up, distant neighbours
of no importance; one notoriously a fool, and the other a
very pious and honest person but such a passionate lover

of the gun that on his own confession he could not have refused an invitation to a shooting-party from the devil himself. X met this manifestation of public opinion with the serenity of an unstained conscience. He refused to be crushed. Yet he must have been a man of deep feeling, because, when his wife took openly the part of her children, he lost his beautiful tranquillity, proclaimed himself heart-broken and drove her out of the house, neglecting in his grief to give her enough time to pack her trunks.

This was the beginning of a lawsuit, an abominable marvel of chicane, which by the use of every legal subterfuge was made to last for many years. It was also the occasion for a display of much kindness and sympathy. All the neighbouring houses flew open for the reception of the homeless. Neither legal aid nor material assistance in the prosecution of the suit was ever wanting. X, on his side, went about shedding tears publicly over his stepchildren's ingratitude and his wife's blind infatuation; but as at the same time he displayed great cleverness in the art of concealing material documents (he was even suspected of having burnt a lot of historically interesting family papers), this scandalous litigation had to be ended by a compromise lest worse should befall. It was settled finally by a surrender, out of the disputed estate, in full satisfaction of all claims, of two villages with the names of which I do not intend to trouble my readers. After this lame and impotent conclusion neither the wife nor the stepsons had anything to say to the man who had presented the world with such a successful example of self-help based on character, determination and industry; and my great-grandmother, her health completely broken down, died a couple of years later in Carlsbad. Legally secured by the decree in the possession of his plunder, X regained his wonted serenity and went on living in the neighbourhood in a comfortable style and in apparent peace of mind. His big shoots were fairly well attended again. He was never tired of assuring people that he bore no grudge for what was past; he protested loudly of his constant affection for his wife and step-children. It was true, he said, that they had tried their best to strip him as naked as a Turkish saint in the decline of his days; and because he had defended himself from spoliation, as anybody else in his place would have done, they had abandoned him now to the horrors of a solitary old age. Nevertheless, his love for them survived these cruel blows. And there might have been some truth in his protestations. Very soon he began to make overtures of friendship to his eldest stepson, my maternal grandfather; and when these were peremptorily rejected, he went on renewing them again and again with characteristic obstinacy. For years he persisted in his efforts at reconciliation, promising my grandfather to execute a will in his favour if he only would be friends again to the extent of calling now and then (it was fairly close neighbourhood for these parts, forty miles or so), or even of putting in an appearance for the great shoot on the name-day. My grandfather was an ardent lover of every sport. His temperament was as free from hardness and animosity as can be imagined. Pupil of the liberal-minded Benedictines who directed the only public school of some standing then in the south, he had also read deeply the authors of the eighteenth century. In him Christian charity was joined to a philosophical indulgence for the failings of human nature. But the memory of these miserably anxious early years, his young man's years robbed of all generous illusions by the cynicism of the sordid lawsuit, stood in the way of forgiveness. He never succumbed to the fascination of the great shoot; and X, his heart set to the last on reconciliation with the draft of the will ready for signature kept by his bedside, died intestate. The fortune thus acquired and augmented by a wise and careful management passed to some distant relatives whom he had never seen and who even did not bear his name.

57

Meantime the blessing of general peace descended upon Europe. Mr. Nicholas B. bidding good-bye to his hospitable relative, the "fearless" Austrian officer, departed from Galicia, and without going near his native place, where the odious lawsuit was still going on, proceeded straight to Warsaw and entered the army of the newly constituted Polish kingdom under the sceptre of Alexander I., Autocrat of all the Russias.

This Kingdom, created by the Vienna Congress as an acknowledgment to a nation of its former independent existence, included only the central provinces of the old Polish patrimony. A brother of the Emperor, the Grand Duke Constantine (Pavlovitch), its Viceroy and Commander-in-Chief, married morganatically to a Polish lady to whom he was fiercely attached, extended this affection to what he called "My Poles" in a capricious and savage manner. Sallow in complexion, with a Tartar physiognomy and fierce little eyes, he walked with his fists clenched, his body bent forward, darting suspicious glances from under an enormous cocked hat. His intelligence was limited and his sanity itself was doubtful. The hereditary taint expressed itself, in his case, not by mystic leanings as in his two brothers, Alexander and Nicholas (in their various ways, for one was mystically liberal and the other mystically autocratic), but by the fury of an uncontrollable temper which generally broke out in disgusting abuse on the parade ground. He was a passionate militarist and an amazing drill-master. He treated his Polish Army as a spoiled child treats a favourite toy, except that he did not take it to bed with him at night. It was not small enough for that. But he played with it all day and every day, delighting in the variety of pretty uniforms and in the fun of incessant drilling. This childish passion, not for war but for mere militarism, achieved a desirable result. The Polish Army, in its equipment, in its armament and in its battlefield efficiency, as then understood, became, by the end of the year 1830, a first-rate tactical instrument. Polish peasantry (not serfs) served in the ranks by enlistment, and the officers belonged mainly to the smaller nobility. Mr. Nicholas B., with his Napoleonic record, had no difficulty in obtaining a lieutenancy, but the promotion in the Polish Army was slow, because, being a separate organisation, it took no part in the wars of the Russian Empire either against Persia or Turkey. Its first campaign, against Russia itself, was to be its last. In 1831, on the outbreak of the Revolution, Mr. Nicholas B. was the senior captain of his regiment. Some time before he had been made head of the remount establishment quartered outside the kingdom in our southern provinces, whence almost all the horses for the Polish cavalry were drawn. For the first time since he went away from home at the age of eighteen to begin his military life by the battle of Friedland, Mr. Nicholas B. breathed the air of the "Border," his native air. Unkind fate was lying in wait for him amongst the scenes of his youth. At the first news of the rising in Warsaw, all the remount establishment, officers, "vets.", and the very troopers, were put promptly under arrest and hurried off in a body beyond the Dnieper to the nearest town in Russia proper. From there they were dispersed to the distant parts of the Empire. On this occasion poor Mr. Nicholas B. penetrated into Russia much farther than he ever did in the times of Napoleonic invasion, if much less willingly. Astrakhan was his destination. He remained there three years, allowed to live at large in the town, but having to report himself every day at noon to the military commandant, who used to detain him frequently for a pipe and a chat. It is difficult to form a just idea of what a chat with Mr. Nicholas B. could have been like. There must have been much compressed rage under his taciturnity, for the commandant communicated to him the news from the theatre of war, and this news was such as it could be, that is, very bad for the Poles. Mr. Nicholas B. received these communications with outward phlegm, but the Russian showed a warm sympathy for his prisoner. "As a soldier myself I understand your feelings. You, of course, would like to be in the thick of it. By heavens! I am fond of you. If it were not for the terms of the military oath I would let you go on my own responsibility. What difference could it make to us, one more or less of you?"

At other times he wondered with simplicity.

"Tell me, Nicholas Stepanovitch" (my grandfather's name was Stephen and the commandant used the Russian form of polite address)—"tell me why is it that you Poles are always looking for trouble? What else could you expect from running up against Russia?"

He was capable, too, of philosophical reflections.

"Look at your Napoleon now. A great man. There is no denying it that he was a great man as long as he was content to thrash those Germans and Austrians and all those nations. But no! He must go to Russia looking for trouble, and what's the consequence? Such as you see me, I have rattled this sabre of mine on the pavements of Paris."

After his return to Poland Mr. Nicholas B. described him as a "worthy man but stupid," whenever he could be induced to speak of the conditions of his exile. Declining the option offered him to enter the Russian Army, he was retired with only half the pension of his rank. His nephew (my uncle and guardian) told me that the first lasting impression on his memory as a child of four was the glad excitement reigning in his parents' house on the day when Mr. Nicholas B. arrived home from his detention in Russia.

Every generation has its memories. The first memories of Mr. Nicholas B. might have been shaped by the events of the last partition of Poland, and he lived long enough to suffer from the last armed rising in 1863, an event which affected the future of all my generation and has coloured my earliest impressions.

His brother, in whose house he had sheltered for some seventeen years his misanthropical timidity before the commonest problems of life, having died in the early fifties, Mr. Nicholas B. had to screw his courage up to the sticking-point and come to some decision as to the future. After a long and agonising hesitation he was persuaded at last to become the tenant of some fifteen hundred acres out of the estate of a friend in the neighbourhood. The terms of the lease were very advantageous, but the retired situation of the village and a plain, comfortable house in good repair were, I fancy, the greatest inducements. He lived there quietly for·about ten years, seeing very few people and taking no part in the public life of the province, such as it could be under an arbitrary, bureaucratic tyranny. His character and his patriotism were above suspicion; but the organisers of the rising in their frequent journeys up and down the province scrupulously avoided coming near his house. It was generally felt that the repose of the old man's last years ought not to be disturbed. Even such intimates as my paternal grandfather, a comrade-in-arms during Napoleon's Moscow campaign and later on a fellow-officer in the Polish Army, refrained from visiting his crony as the date of the outbreak approached. My paternal grandfather's two sons and his only daughter were all deeply involved in the revolutionary work; he himself was of that type of Polish squire whose only ideal of patriotic action was to "get into the saddle and drive them out." But even he agreed that "dear Nicholas must not be worried." All this considerate caution on the part of friends, both conspirators and others, did not prevent Mr. Nicholas B. being made to feel the misfortunes of that ill-omened year.

Less than forty-eight hours after the beginning of the rebellion in that part of the country, a squadron of scouting Cossacks passed through the village and invaded the homestead. Most of them remained, formed between the house and the stables, while several, dismounting, ran-

61

sacked the various outbuildings. The officer in command, accompanied by two men, walked up to the front door. All the blinds on that side were down. The officer told the servant who received him that he wanted to see his master. He was answered that the master was away from home, which was perfectly true.

I follow here the tale as told afterwards by the servant to my grand-uncle's friends and relatives, and as I have heard it repeated.

On receiving this answer the Cossack officer, who had been standing on the porch, stepped into the house.

"Where is the master gone, then?"

"Our master went to J——" (the government town some fifty miles off), "the day before yesterday."

"There are only two horses in the stables. Where are the others?"

"Our master always travels with his own horses" (meaning: not by post). "He will be away a week or more. He was pleased to mention to me that he had to attend to some business in the Civil Court."

While the servant was speaking, the officer looked about the hall. There was a door facing him, a door to the right and a door to the left. The officer chose to enter the room on the left and ordered the blinds to be pulled up. It was Mr. Nicholas B.'s study with a couple of tall bookcases, some pictures on the walls, and so on. Besides the big centre table, with books and papers, there was a quite small writing-table with several drawers, standing between the door and the window in a good light; and at this table my grand-uncle usually sat either to read or write.

On pulling up the blind the servant was startled by the discovery that the whole male population of the village was massed in front, trampling down the flower-beds. There were also a few women amongst them. He was glad to observe the village priest (of the Orthodox Church) coming up the drive. The good man in his haste had tucked up his cassock as high as the top of his boots.

The officer had been looking at the backs of the books in the bookcases. Then he perched himself on the edge of the centre table and remarked easily:

"Your master did not take you to town with him then."

"I am the head servant and he leaves me in charge of the house. It's a strong, young chap that travels with our master. If—God forbid—there was some accident on the road he would be of much more use than I."

Glancing through the window he saw the priest arguing vehemently in the thick of the crowd, which seemed subdued by his interference. Three or four men, however, were talking with the Cossacks at the door.

"And you don't think your master has gone to join the rebels, maybe—eh?" asked the officer.

"Our master would be too old for that, surely. He's well over seventy and he's getting feeble too. It's some years now since he's been on horseback and he can't walk much, either, now."

The officer sat there swinging his leg, very quiet and indifferent. By that time the peasants who had been talking with the Cossack troopers at the door had been permitted to get into the hall. One or two more left the crowd and followed them in. They were seven in all and amongst them the blacksmith, an ex-soldier. The servant appealed deferentially to the officer.

"Won't your honour be pleased to tell the people to go back to their homes? What do they want to push themselves into the house like this for? It's not proper for them to behave like this while our master's away, and I am responsible for everything here."

The officer only laughed a little, and after a while inquired:

"Have you any arms in the house?"

"Yes. We have. Some old things."

"Bring them all here, on to this table."

The servant made another attempt to obtain protection.

"Won't your honour tell these chaps . . . ?"

But the officer looked at him in silence in such a way that he gave it up at once and hurried off to call the pantry-boy to help him collect the arms. Meantime the officer walked slowly through all the rooms in the house, examining them attentively but touching nothing. The peasants in the hall fell back and took off their caps when he passed through. He said nothing whatever to them. When he came back to the study all the arms to be found in the house were lying on the table. There was a pair of big flint-lock holster pistols from Napoleonic times, two cavalry swords, one of the French and the other of the Polish army pattern, with a fowling-piece or two.

The officer, opening the window, flung out pistols, swords and guns, one after another, and his troopers ran to pick them up. The peasants in the hall, encouraged by his manner, had stolen after him into the study. He gave not the slightest sign of being conscious of their existence and, his business being apparently concluded, strode out of the house without a word. Directly he left, the peasants in the study put on their caps and began to smile at each other.

The Cossacks rode away, passing through the yards of the home farm straight into the fields. The priest, still arguing with the peasants, moved gradually down the drive and his earnest eloquence was drawing the silent mob after him, away from the house. This justice must be rendered to the parish priests of the Greek Church that, strangers to the country as they were (being all drawn from the interior of Russia), the majority of them used such influence as they had over their flocks in the cause of peace and humanity. True to the spirit of their calling, they tried to soothe the passions of the excited peasantry and opposed rapine and violence, whenever they could, with all their might. And this conduct they pursued against the express wishes of the authorities. Later on some of them were made to suffer for this disobedience by being removed abruptly to the far north or sent away to Siberian parishes.

The servant was anxious to get rid of the few peasants who had got into the house. What sort of conduct was that, he asked them, towards a man who was only a tenant, had been invariably good and considerate to the villagers for years, and only the other day had agreed to give up two meadows for the use of the village herd? He reminded them, too, of Mr. Nicholas B.'s devotion to the sick in the time of cholera. Every word of this was true and so far effective that the fellows began to scratch their heads and look irresolute. The speaker then pointed at the window, exclaiming: "Look! there's all your crowd going away quietly and you silly chaps had better go after them and pray God to forgive you your evil thoughts."

This appeal was an unlucky inspiration. In crowding clumsily to the window to see whether he was speaking the truth, the fellows overturned the little writing-table. As it fell over a chink of loose coin was heard. "There's money in that thing," cried the blacksmith. In a moment the top of the delicate piece of furniture was smashed and there lay exposed in a drawer eighty half-imperials. Gold coin was a rare sight in Russia even at that time; it put the peasants beside themselves. "There must be more of that in the house and we shall have it," yelled the ex-soldier blacksmith. "This is war-time." The others were already shouting out of the window urging the crowd to come back and help. The priest, abandoned suddenly at the gate, flung his arms up and hurried away so as not to see what was going to happen.

In their search for money that bucolic mob smashed everything in the house, ripping with knives, splitting with hatchets, so that, as the servant said, there were no two pieces of wood holding together left in the whole house. They broke some very fine mirrors, all the windows, and every piece of glass and china. They threw the books and papers out on the lawn and set fire to the heap for the mere fun of the thing, apparently. Absolutely the only one solitary thing which they left whole was a small ivory crucifix, which remained hanging on the wall in the wrecked bedroom above a wild heap of rags, broken mahogany and splintered boards which had been Mr. Nicholas B.'s bedstead. Detecting the servant in the act of stealing away with a japanned tin box, they tore it from him, and because he resisted they threw him out of the dining-room window. The house was on one floor but raised well above the ground, and the fall was so serious that the man remained lying stunned till the cook and a stable-boy ventured forth at dusk from their hiding-places and picked him up. By that time the mob had departed, carrying off the tin box, which they supposed to be full of paper money. Some distance from the house in the middle of a field they broke it open. They found inside documents engrossed on parchment and the two crosses of the Legion of Honour and For Valour. At the sight of these objects, which, the blacksmith explained, were marks of honour given only by the Tsar, they became extremely frightened at what they had done. They threw the whole lot away into a ditch and dispersed hastily.

On learning of this particular loss, Mr. Nicholas B. broke down completely. The mere sacking of his house did not seem to affect him much. While he was still in bed from the shock the two crosses were found and returned to him. It helped somewhat his slow convalescence, but the tin bnox and the parchments, though searched for in all the ditches around, never turned up again. He could not get over the loss of his Legion of Honour Patent, whose preamble, setting forth his services, he knew by heart to the very letter, and after this blow volunteered sometimes to recite, tears standing in his eyes the while.

Its terms haunted him apparently during the last two years of his life to such an extent that he used to repeat them to himself. This is confirmed by the remark made more than once by his old servant to the more intimate friends: "What makes my heart heavy is to hear our master in his room at night walking up and down and praying aloud in the French language."

It must have been somewhat over a year afterwards that I saw Mr. Nicholas B., or, more correctly, that he saw me, for the last time. It was, as I have already said, at the time when my mother had a three-months' leave from exile, which she was spending in the house of her brother, and friends and relations were coming from far and near to do her honour. It is inconceivable that Mr. Nicholas B. should not have been of the number. The little child a few months old he had taken up in his arms on the day of his home-coming after years of war and exile was confessing her faith in national salvation by suffering exile in her turn. I do not know whether he was present on the very day of our departure. I have already admitted that for me he is more especially the man who in his youth had eaten roast dog in the depths of a gloomy forest of snow-loaded pines. My memory cannot place him in any remembered scene. A hooked nose, some sleek white hair, an unrelated evanescent impression of a meagre, slight, rigid figure militarily buttoned up to the throat, is all that now exists on earth of Mr. Nicholas B., only this vague shadow pursued by the memory of his grand-nephew, the last surviving human being, I suppose, of all those he had seen in the course of his taciturn life.

But I remember well the day of our departure back to exile. The elongated, *bizarre*, shabby travelling-carriage with four post-horses, standing before the long front of the house with its eight columns, four on each side of the broad flight of stairs. On the steps, groups of servants, a few relations, one or two friends from the nearest neighbourhood, a perfect silence, on all the faces an air of sober concentration; my grandmother all in black gazing stoically, my uncle giving his arm to my mother down to the carriage in which I had been placed already; at the top of the flight my little cousin in a short skirt of a tartan pattern with a deal of red in it, and like a small princess attended by the women of her own household: the head *gouvernante*, our dear, corpulent Francesca (who had been for thirty years in the service of the B. family), the former nurse, now outdoor attendant, a handsome peasant face wearing a compassionate expression, and the good, ugly Mlle. Durand, the governess, with her black eyebrows meeting over a short thick nose, and a complexion like pale brown paper. Of all the eyes turned towards the carriage, her good-natured eyes only were dropping tears, and it was her sobbing voice alone that broke the silence with an appeal to me: *"N'oublie pas ton français, mon chéri."* In three months, simply by playing with us, she had taught me not only to speak French but to read it as well. She was indeed an excellent playmate. In the distance, halfway down to the great gates, a light, open trap, harnessed with three horses in Russian fashion, stood drawn up on one side with the police captain of the district sitting in it, the vizor of his flat cap with a red band pulled down over his eyes.

It seems strange that he should have been there to watch our going so carefully. Without wishing to treat with levity the just timidities of Imperialists all the world over, I may allow myself the reflection that a woman, practically condemned by the doctors, and a small boy not quite six years old could not be regarded as seriously dangerous even for the largest of conceivable empires saddled with the most sacred of responsibilities. And this good man, I believe, did not think so either.

I learned afterwards why he was present on that day. I don't remember any outward signs, but it seems that, about a month before, my mother became so unwell that there was a doubt whether she could be made fit to travel in the time. In this uncertainty the Governor-General in Kiev was petitioned to grant her a fortnight's extension of stay in her brother's house. No answer whatever was returned to this prayer, but one day at dusk the police-captain of the district drove up to the house and told my uncle's valet, who ran out to meet him, that he wanted to speak with the master in private, at once. Very much impressed (he thought it was going to be an arrest) the servant, "more dead than alive with fright," as he related afterwards, smuggled him through the big drawing-room which was dark (that room was not lighted every evening), on tiptoe, so as not to attract the attention of the ladies in the house, and led him by way of the orangery to my uncle's private apartments.

The policeman, without any preliminaries, thrust a paper into my uncle's hands.

"There. Pray read this. I have no business to show this paper to you. It is wrong of me. But I can't either eat or sleep with such a job hanging over me."

That police-captain, a native of Great Russia, had been for many years serving in the district.

My uncle unfolded and read the document. It was a service order issued from the Governor-General's secretariat, dealing with the matter of the petition and directing the police-captain to disregard all remonstrances and explanations in regard to that illness either from medical men or others, "and if she has not left her brother's house"—it went on to say—"on the morning of the day specified on her permit, you are to despatch her at once under escort, direct" (underlined) "to the prison-hospital in Kiev, where she will be treated as her case demands."

"For God's sake, Mr. B., see that your sister goes away punctually on that day. Don't give me this work to do with a woman—and with one of your family, too. I simply cannot bear to think of it."

He was absolutely wringing his hands. My uncle looked at him in silence.

"Thank you for this warning. I assure you that even if she were dying she would be carried out to the carriage."

"Yes—indeed—and what difference would it make—

travel to Kiev or back to her husband? For she would have to go—death or no death. And mind, Mr. B., I will be here on the day, not that I doubt your promise but because I must. I have got to. Duty. All the same, my trade is not fit for a dog since some of you Poles will persist in rebelling, and all of you have got to suffer for it."

This is the reason why he was there in an open three-horse trap pulled up between the house and the great gates. I regret not being able to give up his name to the scorn of all believers in the rights of conquest, as a reprehensibly sensitive guardian of Imperial greatness. On the other hand, I am in a position to state the name of the Governor-General who signed the order with the marginal note "to be carried out to the letter" in his own handwriting. The gentleman's name was Bezak. A high dignitary, an energetic official, the idol for a time of the Russian Patriotic Press.

Each generation has its memories.

IV

IT must not be supposed that in setting forth the memories of this half-hour between the moment my uncle left the room till we met again at dinner, I am losing sight of *Almayer's Folly*. Having confessed that my first novel was begun in idleness—a holiday task—I think I have also given the impression that it was a much-delayed book. It was never dismissed from my mind, even when the hope of ever finishing it was very faint. Many things came in its way: daily duties, new impressions, old memories. It was not the outcome of a need—the famous need of self-expression which artists find in their search for motives. The necessity which impelled me was a hidden, obscure necessity, a completely masked and unaccountable phenomenon. Or perhaps some idle and frivolous magician (there must be magicians in London) had cast a spell over me through his parlour window as I explored the maze of streets east and west in solitary leisurely walks without chart and compass. Till I began to write that novel I had written nothing but letters, and not very many of these. I never made a note of a fact, of an impression or of an anecdote in my life. The conception of a planned book was entirely outside my mental range when I sat down to write; the ambition of being an author had

never turned up amongst these gracious imaginary exist-
ences one creates fondly for oneself at times in the stillness and immobility of a day-dream: yet it stands clear as
the sun at noonday that from the moment I had done
blackening over the first manuscript page of *Almayer's
Folly* (it contained about two hundred words and this
proportion of words to a page has remained with me
through the fifteen years of my writing life), from the
moment I had, in the simplicity of my heart and the
amazing ignorance of my mind, written that page the die
was cast. Never had Rubicon been more blindly forded,
without invocation to the gods, without fear of men.

That morning I got up from my breakfast, pushing the
chair back, and rang the bell violently, or perhaps I should
say resolutely, or perhaps I should say eagerly, I do not
know. But manifestly it must have been a special ring of
the bell, a common sound made impressive, like the ring-
ing of a bell for the raising of the curtain upon a new
scene. It was an unusual thing for me to do. Generally, I
dawdled over my breakfast and I seldom took the trouble
to ring the bell for the table to be cleared away; but on
that morning for some reason hidden in the general mysteriousness of the event I did not dawdle. And yet I was
not in a hurry. I pulled the cord casually, and while the
faint tinkling somewhere down in the basement went on,
I charged my pipe in the usual way and I looked for the
matchbox with glances distraught indeed but exhibiting,
I am ready to swear, no signs of a fine frenzy. I was
composed enough to perceive after sonme considerable
time the matchbox lying there on the mantelpiece right
under my nose. And all this was beautifully and safely
usual. Before I had thrown down the match my landlady's
daughter appeared with her calm, pale face and an inquis-
itive look, in the doorway. Of late it was the landlady's
daughter who answered my bell. I mention this little fact
with pride, because it proves that during the thirty or
forty days of my tenancy I had produced a favourable

impression. For a fortnight past I had been spared the unattractive sight of the domestic slave. The girls in that Bessborough Gardens house were often changed, but whether short or long, fair or dark, they were always untidy and particularly bedraggled, as if in a sordid version of the fairy tale the ashbin cat had been changed into a maid. I was infinitely sensible of the privilege of being waited on by my landlady's daughter. She was neat if anæmic.

"Will you please clear away all this at once?" I addressed her in convulsive accents, being at the same time engaged in getting my pipe to draw. This, I admit, was an unusual request. Generally on getting up from breakfast I would sit down in the window with a book and let them clear the table when they liked; but if you think that on that morning I was in the least impatient, you are mistaken. I remember that I was perfectly calm. As a matter of fact I was not at all certain that I wanted to write, or that I meant to write, or that I had anything to write about. No, I was not impatient. I lounged between the mantelpiece and the window, not even consciously waiting for the table to be cleared. It was ten to one that before my landlady's daughter was done I would pick up a book and sit down with it all the morning in a spirit of enjoyable indolence. I affirm it with assurance, and I don't even know what were the books then lying about the room. Whatever they were they were not the works of great masters, where the secret of clear thought and exact expression can be found. Since the age of five I have been a great reader, as is not perhaps wonderful in a child who was never aware of learning to read. At ten years of age I had read much of Victor Hugo and other romantics. I had read in Polish and in French, history, voyages, novels; I knew *Gil Blas* and *Don Quixote* in abridged editions; I had read in early boyhood Polish poets and some French poets, but I cannot say what I read on the evening before I began to write myself. I believe it was a novel, and it is

quite possible that it was one of Anthony Trollope's novels. It is very likely. My acquaintance with him was then
very recent. He is one of the English novelists whose
works I read for the first time in English. With men of
European reputation, with Dickens and Walter Scott and
Thackeray, it was otherwise. My first introduction to
English imaginative literature was *Nicholas Nickleby*. It
is extraordinary how well Mrs. Nickleby could chatter
disconnectedly in Polish and the sinister Ralph rage in
that language. As to the Crummles family and the family
of the learned Squeers, it seemed as natural to them as
their native speech. It was, I have no doubt, an excellent
translation. This must have been in the year '70. But I
really believe that I am wrong. That book was not my first
introduction to English literature. My first acquaintance
was (or were) the *The Two Gentlemen of Verona*, and that
in the very MS. of my father's translation. It was during
our exile in Russia, and it must have been less than a year
after my mother's death, because I remember myself in
the black blouse with a white border of my heavy mourn-
ing. We were living together, quite alone, in a small house
on the outskirts of the town of T——. That afternoon,
instead of going out to play in the large yard which we
shared with our landlord, I had lingered in the room in
which my father generally wrote. What emboldened me
to clamber into his chair I am sure I don't know, but a
couple of hours afterwards he discovered me kneeling in
it with my elbows on the table and my head held in both
hands over the MS. of loose pages. I was greatly confused,
expecting to get into trouble. He stood in the doorway
looking at me with some surprise, but the only thing he
said after a moment of silence was:

"Read the page aloud."

Luckily the page lying before me was not overblotted
with erasures and corrections, and my father's handwriting was otherwise extremely legible. When I got to the
end he nodded and I flew out of doors thinking myself

lucky to have escaped reproof for that piece of impulsive audacity. I have tried to discover since the reason of this mildness, and I imagine that all unknown to myself I had earned, in my father's mind, the right to some latitude in my relations with his writing-table. It was only a month before, or perhaps it was only a week before that I had read to him aloud from beginning to end, and to his perfect satisfaction, as he lay on his bed, not being very well at the time, the proofs of his translation of Victor Hugo's *Toilers of the Sea*. Such was my title to consideration, I believe, and also my first introduction to the sea in literature. If I do not remember where, how and when I learned to read, I am not likely to forget the process of being trained in the art of reading aloud. My poor father, an admirable reader himself, was the most exacting of masters. I reflect proudly that I must have read that page of *Two Gentlemen of Verona* tolerably well at the age of eight. The next time I met them was in a five-shilling one-volume edition of the dramatic works of William Shakespeare, read in Falmouth, at odd moments of the day, to the noisy accompaniment of caulkers' mallets driving oakum into the deck-seams of a ship in dry-dock. We had run in, in a sinking condition and with the crew refusing duty after a month of weary battling with the gales of the North Atlantic. Books are an integral part of one's life and my Shakespearean associations are with that first year of our bereavement, the last I spent with my father in exile (he sent me away to Poland to my mother's brother directly he could brace himself for the separation), and with the year of hard gales, the year in which I came nearest to death at sea, first by water and then by fire.

Those things I remember, but what I was reading the day before my writing life began I have forgotten. I have only a vague notion that it might have been one of Trollope's political novels. And I remember, too, the character of the day. It was an autumn day with an opaline atmosphere, a veiled, semi-opaque, lustrous day, with fiery points and flashes of red sunlight on the roofs and windows opposite, while the trees of the square with all their leaves gone were like tracings of India ink on a sheet of tissue paper. It was one of those London days that have the charm of mysterious amenity, of fascinating softness. The effect of opaline mist was often repeated at Bessborough Gardens on account of the nearness to the river.

There is no reason why I should remember that effect more on that day than on any other day, except that I stood for a long time looking out of the window after the landlady's daughter was gone with her spoil of cups and saucers. I heard her put the tray down in the passage and finally shut the door; and still I remained smoking with my back to the room. It is very clear that I was in no haste to take the plunge into my writing life, if as plunge this first attempt may be described. My whole being was steeped deep in the indolence of a sailor away from the sea, the scene of never-ending labour and of unceasing duty. For utter surrender to indolence you cannot beat a sailor ashore when that mood is on him, the mood of absolute irresponsibility tasted to the full. It seems to me that I thought of nothing whatever, but this is an impression which is hardly to be believed at this distance of years. What I am certain of is, that I was very far from thinking of writing a story, though it is possible and even likely that I was thinking of the man Almayer.

I had seen him for the first time some four years before from the bridge of a steamer moored to a rickety little wharf forty miles up, more or less, a Bornean river. It was very early morning, and a slight mist, an opaline mist as in Bessborough Gardens only without the fiery flicks on roof and chimney-pot from the rays of the red London sun, promised to turn presently into a woolly fog. Barring a small dug-out canoe on the river, there was nothing moving within sight. I had just come up yawning from my cabin. The serang and the Malay crew were overhauling the cargo chains and trying the winches; their voices sounded subdued on the deck below and their movements were languid. That tropical daybreak was chilly. The Malay quartermaster, coming up to get something from the lockers on the bridge, shivered visibly. The forests above and below and on the opposite bank looked black and dank; wet dripped from the rigging upon the tightly stretched deck awnings, and it was in the middle of a shuddering yawn that I caught sight of Almayer. He was moving across a patch of burnt grass, a blurred, shadowy shape with the blurred bulk of a house behind him, a low house of mats, bamboos and palm-leaves with a high-pitched roof of grass.

He stepped upon the jetty. He was clad simply in flapping pajamas of cretonne pattern (enormous flowers with yellow petals on a disagreeable blue ground) and a thin cotton singlet with short sleeves. His arms, bare to the elbow, were crossed on his chest. His black hair looked as if it had not been cut for a very long time and a curly wisp of it strayed across his forehead. I had heard of him at Singapore; I had heard of him on board; I had heard of him early in the morning and late at night; I had heard of him at tiffin and at dinner; I had heard of him in a place called Pulo Laut from a half-caste gentleman there, who described himself as the manager of a coal-mine; which sounded civilised and progressive till you heard that the mine could not be worked at present because it was haunted by some particularly atrocious ghosts. I had heard of him in a place called Dongola, in the Island of Celebes, when the Rajah of that little-known seaport (you can get no anchorage there in less than fifteen fathom, which is extremely inconvenient) came on board in a friendly way with only two attendants, and drank bottle after bottle of soda-water on the after-skylight with my good friend and commander Captain C——. At least I heard his name distinctly pronounced several times in a lot of talk in Malay language. Oh, yes, I heard it quite distinctly—

Almayer, Almayer—and saw Captain C—— smile while
the fat, dingy Rajah laughed audibly. To hear a Malay
Rajah laugh outright is a rare experience, I can asssure
you. And I overheard more of Almayer's name amongst
our deck passengers (mostly wandering traders of good
repute) as they sat all over the ship—each man fenced
round with bundles and boxes—on mats, on pillows, on
quilts, on billets of wood, conversing of Island affairs.
Upon my word, I heard the mutter of Almayer's name
faintly at midnight, while making my way aft from the
bridge to look at the patent taffrail-log tinkling its quar-
ter-miles in the great silence of the sea. I don't mean to
say that our passengers dreamed aloud of Almayer, but it
is indubitable that two of them at least, who could not
sleep apparently and were trying to charm away the trouble of insomnia by a little whispered talk at that ghostly
hour, were referring in some way or other to Almayer. It
was really impossible on board that ship to get away
definitely from Almayer; and a very small pony tied up
forward and whisking its tail inside the galley, to the
great embarrassment of our Chinaman cook, was destined for Almayer. What he wanted with a pony goodness
only knows, since I am perfectly certain he could not ride
it; but here you have the man, ambitious, aiming at the
grandiose, importing a pony, whereas in the whole settle-
ment at which he used to shake daily his impotent fist,
there was only one path that was practicable for a pony: a
quarter of a mile at most, hedged in by hundreds of square
leagues of virgin forest. But who knows? The importation
of that Bali pony might have been part of some deep
scheme, of some diplomatic plan, of some hopeful in-
trigue. With Almayer one could never tell. He governed
his conduct by considerations removed from the obvious,
by incredible assumptions, which rendered his logic im-
penetrable to any reasonable persons. I learned all this
later. That morning, seeing the figure in pyjamas moving
in the mist, I said to myself: "That's the man."

He came quite close to the ship's side and raised a harassed countenace, round and flat, with that curl of black hair over the forehead and a heavy, pained glance.

"Good morning."

"Good morning."

He looked hard at me: I was a new face, having just replaced the chief mate he was accustomed to see; and I think that this novelty inspired him, as things generally did, with deep-seated mistrust.

"Didn't expect you in till this evening," he remarked suspiciously.

I don't know why he should have been aggrieved, but he seemed to be. I took pains to explain to him that having picked up the beacon at the mouth of the river just before dark and the tide serving, Captain C—— was enabled to cross the bar and there was nothing to prevent him going up the river at night.

"Captain C—— knows this river like his own pocket," I concluded discursively, trying to get on terms.

"Better," said Almayer.

Leaning over the rail of the bridge I looked at Almayer, who looked down at the wharf in aggrieved thought. He shuffled his feet a little; he wore straw slippers with thick soles. The morning fog had thickened considerably. Everything round us dripped: the derricks, the rails, every single rope in the ship—as if a fit of crying had come upon the universe.

Almayer again raised his head and, in the accents of a man accustomed to the buffets of evil fortune, asked hardly audibly: "I suppose you haven't got such a thing as a pony on board?"

I told him almost in a whisper, for he attuned my communications to his minor key, that we had such a thing as a pony, and I hinted, as gently as I could, that he was confoundedly in the way too. I was very anxious to have him landed before I began to handle the cargo. Almayer remained looking up at me for a long while with incredulous and melancholy eyes as though it were not a safe thing to believe my statement. This pathetic mistrust in the favourable issue of any sort of affair touched me deeply, and I added:

"He doesn't seem a bit worse for the passage. He's a nice pony, too."

Almayer was not to be cheered up; for all answer he cleared his throat and looked down again at his feet. I tried to close with him on another track.

"By Jove!" I said. "Aren't you afraid of catching pneumonia or bronchitis or something, walking about in a singlet in such a wet fog?"

He was not to be propitiated by a show of interest in his health. His answer was a sinister "No fear," as much as to say that even that way of escape from inclement fortune was closed to him.

"I just came down . . ." he mumbled after a while.

"Well, then, now you're here I will land that pony for you at once and you can lead him home. I really don't want him on deck. He's in the way."

Almayer seemed doubtful. I insisted:

"Why, I will just swing him out and land him on the wharf right in front of you. I'd much rather do it before the hatches are off. The little devil may jump down the hold or do some other deadly thing."

"There's a halter?" postulated Almayer.

"Yes, of course there's a halter." And without waiting any more I leaned over the bridge rail.

"Serang, land Tuan Almayer's pony."

The cook hastened to shut the door of the galley and a moment later a great scuffle began on deck. The pony kicked with extreme energy, the kalashes skipped out of the way, the serang issued many orders in a cracked voice. Suddenly the pony leaped upon the fore-hatch. His little hoofs thundered tremendously; he plunged and reared. He had tossed his mane and his forelock into a state of amazing wildness, he dilated his nostrils, bits of foam flecked

80

his broad little chest, his eyes blazed. He was something under eleven hands, he was fierce, terrible, angry, war-like, he said ha! ha! distinctly, he raged and thumped— and sixteen able-bodied kalashes stood round him like disconcerted nurses round a spoilt and passionate child. He whisked his tail incessantly; he arched his pretty neck; he was perfectly delightful; he was charmingly naughty. There was not an atom of vice in that performance; no savage baring of teeth and laying back of ears. On the contrary, he pricked them forward in a comically aggressive manner. He was totally unmoral and lovable; I would have liked to give him bread, sugar, carrots. But life is a stern thing and the sense of duty the only safe guide. So I steeled my heart and from my elevated position on the bridge I ordered the men to fling themselves upon him in a body.

The elderly serang, emitting a strange inarticulate cry, gave the example. He was an excellent petty officer—very competent indeed, and a moderate opium smoker. The rest of them in one great rush smothered that pony. They hung on to his ears, to his mane, to his tail; they lay in piles across his back, seventeen in all. The carpenter, seizing the hook of the cargo-chain, flung himself on the top of them. A very satisfactory petty officer too, but he stuttered. Have you ever heard a light-yellow, lean, sad, earnest Chinaman stutter in pidgin-English? It's very weird indeed. He made the eighteenth. I could not see the pony at all; but from the swaying and heaving of that heap of men I knew that there was something alive inside.

From the wharf Almayer hailed in quavering tones: "Oh, I say!"

Where he stood he could not see what was going on on deck unless perhaps the tops of the men's heads; he could only hear the scuffle, the mighty thuds as if the ship were being knocked to pieces. I looked over: "What is it?"

"Don't let them break his legs," he entreated me plaintively.

81

"Oh, nonsense! He's all right now. He can't move."

By that time the cargo-chain had been hooked to the broad canvas belt round the pony's body, the kalashes sprang off simultaneously in all directions, rolling over each other, and the worthy serang, making a dash behind the winch, turned the steam on.

"Steady!" I yelled, in great apprehension of seeing the animal snatched up to the very head of the derrick.

On the wharf Almayer shuffled his straw slippers uneasily. The rattle of the winch stopped, and in a tense, impressive silence that pony began to swing across the deck.

How limp he was! Directly he felt himself in the air he relaxed every muscle in a most wonderful manner. His four hoofs knocked together in a bunch, his head hung down, and his tail remained pendent in a nerveless and absolute immobility. He reminded me vividly of the pathetic little sheep which hangs on the collar of the Order of the Golden Fleece. I had no idea that anything in the shape of a horse could be so limp as that, either living or dead. His wild mane hung down lumpily, a mere mass of inanimate horsehair; his aggressive ears had collapsed, but as he went swaying slowly across the front of the bridge I noticed an astute gleam in his dreamy, half-closed eye. A trustworthy quartermaster, his glance anxious and his mouth on the broad grin, was easing over the derrick watchfully. I superintended, greatly interested.

"So! That will do."

The derrick-head stopped. The kalashes lined the rail. The rope of the halter hung perpendicular and motionless like a bell-pull in front of Almayer. Everything was very still. I suggested amicably that he should catch hold of the rope and mind what he was about. He extended a provokingly casual and superior hand.

"Look out, then! Lower away!"

Almayer gathered in the rope intelligently enough, but

when the pony's hoofs touched the wharf he gave way all at once to a most foolish optimism. Without pausing, without thinking, almost without looking, he disengaged the hook suddenly from the sling, and the cargo-chain, after hitting the pony's quarters, swung back against the ship's side with a noisy, rattling slap. I suppose I must have blinked. I know I missed something, because the next thing I saw was Almayer lying flat on his back on the jetty. He was alone.

Astonishment deprived me of speech long enough to give Almayer time to pick himself up in a leisurely and painful manner. The kalashes lining the rail all had their mouths open. The mist flew in the light breeze, and it had come over quite thick enough to hide the shore completely.

"How on earth did you manage to let him get away?" I asked, scandalised.

Almayer looked into the smarting palm of his right hand, but did not answer my inquiry.

"Where do you think he will get to?" I cried. "Are there any fences anywhere in this fog? Can he bolt into the forest? What's to be done now?"

Almayer shrugged his shoulders.

"Some of my men are sure to be about. They will get hold of him sooner or later."

"Sooner or later! That's all very fine, but what about my canvas sling?—he's carried it off. I want it now, at once, to land two Celebes cows."

Since Dongola we had on board a pair of the pretty little island cattle in addition to the pony. Tied up on the other side of the fore-deck they had been whisking their tails into the other door of the galley. These cows were not for Almayer, however, they were invoiced to Abdullah bin Selim, his enemy. Almayer's disregard of my requirements was complete.

"If I were you I would try to find out where he's gone," I insisted. "Hadn't you better call your men together or something? He will throw himself down and cut his knees. He may even break a leg, you know."

But Almayer, plunged in abstracted thought, did not seem to want that pony any more. Amazed at this sudden indifference, I turned all hands out on shore to hunt for him on my own account, or, at any rate, to hunt for the canvas sling which he had round his body. The whole crew of the steamer, with the exception of firemen and engineers, rushed up the jetty past the thoughtful Almayer and vanished from my sight. The white fog swallowed them up; and again there was a deep silence that seemed to extend for miles up and down the stream. Still taciturn, Almayer started to climb on board, and I went down from the bridge to meet him on the after-deck.

"Would you mind telling the captain that I want to see him very particularly?" he asked me in a low tone, letting his eyes stray all over the place.

"Very well. I will go and see."

With the door of his cabin wide open Captain C——, just back from the bath-room, big and broad-chested, was brushing his thick, damp, iron-grey hair with two large brushes.

"Mr. Almayer told me he wanted to see you very particularly, sir."

Saying these words I smiled. I don't know why I smiled except that it seemed absolutely impossible to mention Almayer's name without a smile of a sort. It had not to be necessarily a mirthful smile. Turning his head towards me Captain C—— smiled too, rather joylessly.

"The pony got away from him—eh?"

"Yes, sir. He did."

"Where is he?"

"Goodness only knows."

"No. I mean Almayer. Let him come along."

The captain's stateroom opening straight on deck under the bridge, I had only to beckon from the doorway to Almayer, who had remained aft, with downcast eyes, on

the very spot where I had left him. He strolled up mood-
ily, shook hands, and at once asked permission to shut
the cabin door.

"I have a pretty story to tell you," were the last words
I heard. The bitterness of tone was remarkable.

I went away from the door, of course. For the moment
I had no crew on board; only the Chinaman carpenter,
with a canvas bag hung round his neck and a hammer in
his hand, roamed about the empty decks knocking out
the wedges of the hatches and dropping them into the bag
conscientiously. Having nothing to do, I joined our two
engineers at the door of the engine-room. It was near
breakfast-time.

"He's turned up early, hasn't he?" commented the second engineer, and smiled indifferently. He was an abstemious man with a good digestion and a placid, reasonable
view of life even when hungry.

"Yes," I said. "Shut up with the old man. Some very
particular business."

"He will spin him a damned endless yarn," observed
the chief engineer.

He smiled rather sourly. He was a dyspeptic and suf-
fered from gnawing hunger in the morning. The second
smiled broadly, a smile that made two vertical folds on
his shaven cheeks. And I smiled too, but I was not exactly
amused. In that man, whose name apparently could not
be uttered anywhere in the Malay Archipelago without a
smile, there was nothing amusing whatever. That morning he breakfasted with us silently, looking mostly into
his cup. I informed him that my men came upon his pony
capering in the fog on the very brink of the eight-foot-deep
well in which he kept his store of guttah. The cover was
off, with no one near by, and the whole of my crew just
missed going heels over head into that beastly hole. Juru-
mudi Itam, our best quartermaster, deft at fine needle-
work, he who mended the ship's flags and sewed buttons
on our coats, was disabled by a kick on the shoulder.

Both remorse and gratitude seemed foreign to Almayer's character. He mumbled:

"Do you mean that pirate fellow?"

"What pirate fellow? The man has been in the ship eleven years," I said indignantly.

"It's his looks," Almayer muttered for all apology.

The sun had eaten up the fog. From where we sat under the after-awning we could see in the distance the pony tied up in front of Almayer's house, to a post of the verandah. We were silent for a long time. All at once Almayer, alluding evidently to the subject of his conversation in the captain's cabin, exclaimed anxiously across the table.

"I really don't know what I can do now!"

Captain C—— only raised his eyebrows at him, and got up from his chair. We dispersed to our duties, but Almayer, half-dressed as he was in his cretonne pajamas and the thin cotton singlet, remained on board, lingering near the gangway as though he could not make up his mind whether to go home or stay with us for good. Our Chinaman boys gave him side glances as they went to and fro; and Ah Sing, our young chief steward, the handsomest and most sympathetic of Chinamen, catching my eye, nodded knowingly at his burly back. In the course of the morning I approached him for a moment.

"Well, Mr. Almayer," I addressed him easily, "you haven't started on your letters yet."

We had brought him his mail and he had held the bundle in his hand ever since we got up from breakfast. He glanced at it when I spoke and, for a moment, it looked as if he were on the point of opening his fingers and letting the whole lot fall overboard. I believe he was tempted to do so. I shall never forget that man afraid of his letters.

"Have you been long out of Europe?" he asked me.

"Not very. Not quite eight months," I told him. "I left

86

a ship in Samarang with a hurt back and have been in the hospital in Singapore some weeks."

He sighed.

"Trade is very bad here."

"Indeed!"

"Hopeless! . . . See these geese?"

With the hand holding the letters he pointed out to me what resembled a patch of snow creeping and swaying across the distant part of his compound. It disappeared behind some bushes.

"The only geese on the East Coast," Almayer informed me in a perfunctory mutter without a spark of faith, hope or pride. Thereupon, with the same absence of any sort of sustaining spirit, he declared his intention to select a fat bird and send him on board for us not later than next day.

I had heard of these largesses before. He conferred a goose as if it were a sort of Court decoration given only to the tried friends of the house. I had expected more pomp in the ceremony. The gift had surely its special quality, multiple and rare. From the only flock on the East Coast! He did not make half enough of it. That man did not understand his opportunities. However, I thanked him at some length.

"You see," he interrupted abruptly in a very peculiar tone, "the worst of this country is that one is not able to realise . . . it's impossible to realise . . ." His voice sank into a languid mutter. "And when one has very large interests . . . very important interests . . ." he finished faintly . . . "up the river."

We looked at each other. He astonished me by giving a start and making a very queer grimace.

"Well, I must be off," he burst out hurriedly. "So long!"

At the moment of stepping over the gangway he checked himself, though, to give me a mumbled invitation to dine at his house that evening with my captain, an invitation which I accepted. I don't think it could have been possible for me to refuse.

I like the worthy folk who will talk to you of the exercise of free will "at any rate for practical purposes." Free, is it? For practical purposes! Bosh! How could I have refused to dine with that man? I did not refuse simply because I could not refuse. Curiosity, a healthy desire for a change of cooking, common civility, the talk and the smiles of the previous twenty days, every condition of my existence at that moment and place made irresistibly for acceptance; and, crowning all that, there was ignorance, the ignorance, I say, the fatal want of fore-knowledge to counterbalance these imperative conditions of the problem. A refusal would have appeared perverse and insane. Nobody unless a surly lunatic would have refused. But if I had not got to know Almayer pretty well it is almost certain there would never have been a line of mine in print.

I accepted then—and I am paying yet the price of my sanity. The possessor of the only flock of geese on the East Coast is responsible for the existence of some fourteen volumes, so far. The number of geese he had called into being under adverse climatic conditions was considerably more than fourteen. The tale of volumes will never overtake the counting of heads, I am safe to say; but my ambitions point not exactly that way, and whatever the pangs the toil of writing has cost me I have always thought kindly of Almayer.

I wonder, had he known anything of this, what his attitude would have been? This is something not to be discovered in this world. But if we ever meet in the Elysian Fields—where I cannot depict him to myself otherwise than attended in the distance by his flock of geese (birds sacred to Jupiter)—and he addresses me in the stillness of that passionless region, neither light nor darkness, neither sound nor silence, and heaving endlessly with billowy mists from the impalpable muiltitudes of the swarming dead, I think I know what answer to make.

I would say, after listening courteously to the unvibrating tone of his measured remonstrances, which should not disturb, of course, the solemn eternity of stillness in the least—I would say something like this:

"It is true, Almayer, that in the world below I have converted your name to my own uses. But that is a very small larceny. What's in a name, O Shade? If so much of your old mortal weakness clings to you yet as to make you feel aggrieved (it was the note of your earthly voice, Almayer), then, I entreat you, seek speech without delay with our sublime fellow-Shade—with him whom, in his transient existence as a poet, commented upon the smell of the rose. He will comfort you. You came to me stripped of all prestige by men's queer smiles and the disrespectful chatter of every vagrant trader in the Islands. Your name was the common property of the winds: it, as it were, floated naked over the waters about the Equator. I wrapped round its unhonoured form the royal mantle of the tropics and have essayed to put into the hollow sound the very anguish of paternity—feats which you did not demand from me—but remember that all the toil and all the pain were mine. In your earthly life you haunted me, Almayer. Consider that this was taking a great liberty. Since you were always complaining of being lost to the world, you should remember that if I had not believed enough in your existence to let you haunt my rooms in Bessborough Gardens you would have been much more lost. You affirm that had I been capable of looking at you with a more perfect detachment and a greater simplicity, I might have perceived better the inward marvellousness which, you insist, attended your career upon that tiny pin-point of light, hardly visible, far, far below us, where both our graves lie. No doubt! But reflect, O complaining Shade! that this was not so much my fault as your crowning misfortune. I believed in you in the only way it was possible for me to believe. It was not worthy of your merits? So be it. But you were always an unlucky man, Almayer. Nothing was ever quite worthy of you. What made you so real to me was that you held this lofty theory with some force of conviction and with an admirable consistency."

It is with some such words translated into the proper shadowy expressions that I am prepared to placate Almayer in the Elysian Abode of Shades, since it has come to pass that having parted many years ago, we are never to meet again in this world.

V

IN the career of the most unliterary of writers, in the sense that literary ambition had never entered the world of his imagination, the coming into existence of the first book is quite an inexplicable event. In my own case I cannot trace it back to any mental or psychological cause which one could point out and hold to. The greatest of my gifts being a consummate capacity for doing nothing, I cannot even point to boredom as a rational stimulus for taking up a pen. The pen at any rate was there, and there is nothing wonderful in that. Everybody keeps a pen (the cold steel of our days) in his rooms in this enlightened age of penny stamps and halfpenny postcards. In fact, this was the epoch when by means of postcard and pen Mr. Gladstone had made the reputation of a novel or two. And I too had a pen rolling about somewhere—the seldom-used, the reluctantly taken-up pen of a sailor ashore, the pen rugged with the dried ink of abandoned attempts, of answers delayed longer than decency permitted, of letters begun with infinite reluctance and put off suddenly till next day—till next week as likely as not! The neglected, uncared-for pen, flung away at the slightest provocation, and under the stress of dire necessity hunted for without enthusiasm, in a perfunctory, grumpy worry, in the

"Where the devil *is* the beastly thing gone to?" ungra-
cious spirit. Where indeed! It might have been reposing
behind the sofa for a day or so. My landlady's anæmic
daughter (as Ollendorff would have expressed it), though
commendably neat, had a lordly, careless manner of ap-
proaching her domestic duties. Or it might even be resting delicately poised on its point by the side of the table-
leg, and when picked up show a gaping inefficient beak
which would have discouraged any man of literary in-
stincts. But not me! "Never mind. This will do."

O days without guile! If anybody had told me then that
a devoted household, having a generally exaggerated idea
of my talents and importance, would be put into a state of
tremor and flurry by the fuss I would make because of a
suspicion that somebody had touched my sacrosanct pen
of authorship, I would have never deigned as much as the
contemptuous smile of unbelief. There are imaginings
too unlikely for any kind of notice, too wild for indulgence itself, too absurd for a smile. Perhaps, had that seer
of the future been a friend, I should have been secretly
saddened. "Alas!" I would have thought, looking at him
with an unmoved face, "the poor fellow is going mad."

I would have been, without doubt, saddened; for in this
world where the journalists read the signs of the sky, and
the wind of heaven itself, blowing where it listeth, does
so under the prophetical management of the Meteorolog-
ical Office, but where the secret of human hearts cannot
be captured either by prying or praying, it was infinitely
more likely that the sanest of my friends should nurse the
germ of incipient madness than that I should turn into a
writer of tales.

To survey with wonder the changes of one's own self is
a fascinating pursuit for idle hours. The field is so wide,
the surprises so varied, the subject so full of unprofitable
but curious hints as to the work of unseen forces, that one
does not weary easily of it. I am not speaking here of
megalomaniacs who rest uneasy under the crown of their

unbounded conceit—who really never rest in this world, and when out of it go on fretting and fuming on the straitened circumstances of their last habitation, where all men must lie in obscure equality. Neither am I thinking of those ambitious minds who, always looking forward to some aim of aggrandisement, can spare no time for a detached, impersonal glance upon themselves.

And that's a pity. They are unlucky. These two kinds, together with the much larger band of the totally unimaginative, of those unfortunate beings in whose empty and unseeing gaze (as a great French writer has put it) "the whole universe vanishes into blank nothingness," miss, perhaps, the true task of us men whose day is short on this earth, the abode of conflicting opinions. The ethical view of the universe involves us at last in so many cruel and absurd contradictions, where the last vestiges of faith, hope, charity, and even of reason itself, seem ready to perish, that I have come to suspect that the aim of creation cannot be ethical at all. I would fondly believe that its object is purely spectacular: a spectacle for awe, love, adoration, or hate, if you like, but in this view—and in this view alone—never for despair! Those visions, delicious or poignant, are a moral end in themselves. The rest is our affair—the laughter, the tears, the tenderness, the indignation, the high tranquillity of a steeled heart, the detached curiosity of a subtle mind—that's our affair! And the unwearied self-forgetful attention to every phase of the living universe reflected in our consciousness may be our appointed task on this earth. A task in which fate has perhaps engaged nothing of us except our conscience, gifted with a voice in order to bear true testimony to the visible wonder, the haunting terror, the infinite passion and the illimitable serenity; to the supreme law and the abiding mystery of the sublime spectacle.

Chi lo sà! It may be true. In this view there is room for every religion except for the inverted creed of impiety, the mask and cloak of arid despair; for every joy and every

93

sorrow, for every fair dream, for every charitable hope.
The great aim is to remain true to the emotions called out
of the deep encircled by the firmament of stars, whose
infinite numbers and awful distance may move us to
laughter or tears (was it the Walrus or the Carpenter, in
the poem, who "wept to see such quantities of sand"?), or,
again, to a properly steeled heart, may matter nothing at
all.

The casual quotation, which had suggested itself out of
a poem full of merit, leads me to remark that in the
conception of a purely spectacular universe, where inspiration of every sort has a rational existence, the artist of
every kind finds a natural place; and amongst them the
poet as the seer *par excellence*. Even the writer of prose,
who in his less noble and more toilsome task should be a
man with the steeled heart, is worthy of a place, providing
he looks on with undimmed eyes and keeps laughter out
of his voice, let who will laugh or cry. Yes! Even he, the
prose artist of fiction, which after all is but truth often
dragged out of a well and clothed in the painted robe of
imaged phrases—even he has his place amongst kings,
demagogues, priests, charlatans, dukes, giraffes, Cabinet
Ministers, Fabians, bricklayers, apostles, ants, scientists,
Kaffirs, soldiers, sailors, elephants, lawyers, dandies, mi-
crobes and constellations of a universe whose amazing
spectacle is a moral end in itself.

Here I perceive (speaking without offence) the reader
assuming a subtle expression, as if the cat were out of the
bag. I take the novelist's freedom to observe the reader's
mind formulating the exclamation, "That's it! The fellow
talks *pro domo.*"

Indeed it was not the intention! When I shouldered the
bag I was not aware of the cat inside. But, after all, why
not? The fair courtyards of the House of Art are thronged
by many humble retainers. And there is no retainer so
devoted as he who is allowed to sit on the doorstep. The
fellows who have got inside are apt to think too much of

themselves. This last remark, I beg to state, is not mali-
cious within the definition of the law of libel. It's fair
comment on a matter of public interest. But never mind.
Promo domo. So be it. For his house *tant que vous vou-
drez.* And yet in truth I was by no means anxious to
justify my existence. The attempt would have been not
only needless and absurd but almost inconceivable, in a
purely spectacular universe, where no such disagreeable
necessity can possibly arise. It is sufficient for me to say
(and I am saying it at some length in these pages): *J'ai
vécu.* I have existed, obscure amongst the wonders and
terrors of my times, as the Abbé Sieyès, the original ut-
terer of the quoted words, had managed to exist through
the violences, the crimes, and the enthusiasms of the
French Revolution. *J'ai vécu,* as I apprehend most of us
manage to exist, missing all along the varied forms of
destruction by a hair's-breadth, saving my body, that's
clear, and perhaps my soul also, but not without some
damage here and there to the fine edge of my conscience,
that heirloom of the ages, of the race, of the group, of the
family, colourable and plastic, fashioned by the words,
the looks, the acts, and even by the silences and absten-
tions surrounding one's childhood; tinged in a complete
scheme of delicate shades and crude colours by the inher-
ited traditions, beliefs, or prejudices—unaccountable, des-
potic, persuasive, and often, in its texture, romantic.

And often romantic! . . . The matter in hand, however,
is to keep these reminiscences from turning into confessions, a form of literary activity discredited by Jean Jacques Rousseau on account of the extreme thoroughness
he brought to the work of justifying his own existence; for
that such was his purpose is palpably, even grossly, visible to an unprejudiced eye. But then, you see, the man
was not a writer of fiction. He was an artless moralist, as
is clearly demonstrated by his anniversaries being cele-
brated with marked emphasis by the heirs of the French
Revolution, which was not a political movement at all,

95

but a great outburst of morality. He had no imagination, as the most casual perusal of *Émile* will prove. He was no novelist, whose first virtue is the exact understanding of the limits traced by the reality of his time to the play of his invention. Inspiration comes from the earth, which has a past, a history, a future, not from the cold and immutable heaven. A writer of imaginative prose (even more than any other sort of artist) stands confessed in his works. His conscience, his deeper sense of things, lawful and unlawful, gives him his attitude before the world. Indeed, everyone who puts pen to paper for the reading of strangers (unless a moralist, who, generally speaking, has no conscience except the one he is at pains to produce for the use of others) can speak of nothing else. It is M. Anatole France, the most eloquent and just of French prose-writers, who says that we must recognise at last that, "failing the resolution to hold our peace, we can only talk of ourselves."

This remark, if I remember rightly, was made in the course of a sparring match with the late Ferdinand Brunetière over the principles and rules of literary criticism. As was fitting for a man to whom we owe the memorable saying, "The good critic is he who relates the adventures of his soul amongst masterpieces," M. Anatole France maintained that there were no rules and no principles. And that may be very true. Rules, principles and standards die and vanish every day. Perhaps they are all dead and vanished by this time. These, if ever, are the brave free days of destroyed landmarks, while the ingenious minds are busy inventing the forms of the new beacons which, it is consoling to think, will be set up presently in the old places. But what is interesting to a writer is the possession of an inward certitude that literary criticism will never die, for man (so variously defined) is, before everything else, a critical animal. And, as long as distinguished minds are ready to treat it in the spirit of high adventure, literary criticism shall appeal to us with all the charm and wisdom of a well-told tale of personal experience.

For Englishmen especially, of all the races of the earth, a task, any task, undertaken in an adventurous spirit acquires the merit of romance. But the critics as a rule exhibit but little of an adventurous spirit. They take risks, of course—one can hardly live without that. The daily bread is served out to us (however sparingly) with a pinch of salt. Otherwise one would get sick of the diet one prays for, and that would be not only improper, but impious. From impiety of that or any other kind—save us! An ideal of reserved manner, adhered to from a sense of proprieties, from shyness, perhaps, or caution, or simply from weariness, induces, I suspect, some writers of criticism to conceal the adventurous side of their calling, and then the criticism becomes a mere "notice," as it were the relation of a journey where nothing but the distances and the geology of a new country should be set down; the glimpses of strange beasts, the dangers of flood and field, the hair's-breadth escapes, and the sufferings (oh, the sufferings too! I have no doubt of the sufferings) of the traveller being carefully kept out; no shady spot, no fruitful plant being ever mentioned either; so that the whole performance looks like a mere feat of agility on the part of a trained pen running in a desert. A cruel spectacle—a most deplorable adventure. "Life," in the words of an immortal thinker of, I should say, bucolic origin, but whose perishable name is lost to the worship of posterity—"life is not all beer and skittles." Neither is the writing of novels. It isn't really. *Je vous donne ma parole d'honneur* that it—is—not. Not *all*. I am thus emphatic because some years ago, I remember, the daughter of a general. . .

Sudden revelations of the profane world must have come now and then to hermits in their cells, to the cloistered monks of middle ages, to lonely sages, men of science, reformers; the revelations of the world's superficial judgment, shocking to the souls concentrated upon their

97

own bitter labour in the cause of sanctity, or of knowledge, or of temperance, let us say, or of art, if only the art of cracking jokes or playing the flute. And thus the general's daughter came to me—or I should say one of the general's daughters did. There were three of these bachelor ladies, of nicely graduated ages, who held a neighbouring farmhouse in a united and more or less military occupation. The eldest warred against the decay of manners in the village children, and executed frontal attacks upon the village mothers for the conquest of courtesies. It sounds futile, but it was really a war for an idea. The second skirmished and scouted all over the country; and it was that one who pushed a reconnaissance right to my very table—I mean the one who wore stand-up collars. She was really calling upon my wife in the soft spirit of afternoon friendliness, but with her usual martial determination. She marched into my room swinging her stick ... but no—I mustn't exaggerate. It is not my specialty. I am not a humoristic writer. In all soberness, then, all I am certain of is that she had a stick to swing.

No ditch or wall encompassed my abode. The window was open; the door too stood open to that best friend of my work, the warm, still sunshine of the wide fields. They lay around me infinitely helpful, but truth to say I had not known for weeks whether the sun shone upon the earth and whether the stars above still moved on their appointed courses. I was just then giving up some days of my allotted span to the last chapters of *Nostromo*, a tale of an imaginary (but true) seaboard, which is still mentioned now and again, and indeed kindly, sometimes in conjunction with the word "failure" and sometimes in conjunction with the word "astonishing." I have no opinion on this discrepancy. It's the sort of difference that can never be settled. All I know, is that, for twenty months, neglecting the common joys of life that fall to the lot of the humblest on this earth, I had, like the prophet of old, "wrestled with the Lord" for my creation, for the headlands of the coast, for the darkness of the Placid Gulf, the light on the snows, the clouds on the sky, and for the breath of life that had to be blown into the shapes of men and women, of Latin and Saxon, of Jew and Gentile. These are, perhaps, strong words, but it is difficult to character-ise otherwise the intimacy and the strain of a creative effort in which mind and will and conscience are engaged to the full, hour after hour, day after day, away from the world, and to the exclusion of all that makes life really lovable and gentle—something for which a material par-allel can only be found in the everlasting sombre stress of the westward winter passage round Cape Horn. For that too is the wrestling of men with the might of their Cre-ator, in a great isolation from the world, without the amenities and consolations of life, a lonely struggle under a sense of overmatched littleness, for no reward that could be adequate, but for the mere winning of a longitude. Yet a certain longitude, once won, cannot be disputed. The sun and the stars and the shape of your earth are the witnesses of your gain; whereas a handful of pages, no matter how much you have made them your own, are at best but an obscure and questionable spoil. Here they are. "Failure"—"Astonishing": take your choice; or perhaps both, or neither—a mere rustle and flutter of pieces of paper settling down in the night, and undistinguishable, like the snowflakes of a great drift destined to melt away in sunshine.

"How do you do?"

It was the greeting of the general's daughter. I had heard nothing—no rustle, no footsteps. I had felt only a mo-ment before a sort of premonition of evil; I had the sense of an inauspicious presence—just that much warning and no more; and then came the sound of the voice and the jar as of a terrible fall from a great height—a fall, let us say, from the highest of the clouds floating in gentle proces-sion over the fields in the faint westerly air of that July afternoon. I picked myself up quickly, of course; in other words, I jumped up from my chair stunned and dazed, every nerve quivering with the pain of being uprooted out of one world and flung down into another—perfectly civil.

"Oh! How do you do? Won't you sit down?"

That's what I said. This horrible but, I assure you, perfectly true reminiscence tells you more than a whole volume of confessions *à la* Jean Jacques Rousseau would do. Observe! I didn't howl at her, or start upsetting furniture, or throw myself on the floor and kick, or allow myself to hint in any other way at the appalling magnitude of the disaster. The whole world of Costaguana (the country, you may remember, of my seaboard tale), men, women, headlands, houses, mountains, town, *campo,* (there was not a single brick, stone, or grain of sand of its soil I had not placed in position with my own hands); all the history, geography, politics, finance; the wealth of Charles Gould's silver-mine, and the splendour of the magnificent Capataz de Cargadores, whose name, cried out in the night (Dr. Monygham heard it pass over his head—in Linda Viola's voice), dominated even after death the dark gulf containing his conquests of treasure and love—all that had come down crashing about my ears. I felt I could never pick up the pieces—and in that very moment I was saying, "Won't you sit down?"

The sea is strong medicine. Behold what the quarter-deck training even in a merchant ship will do! This episode should give you a new view of the English and Scots seamen (a much-caricatured folk) who had the last say in the formation of my character. One is nothing if not modest, but in this disaster I think I have done some honour to their simple teaching: "Won't you sit down?" Very fair; very fair indeed. She sat down. Her amused glance strayed all over the room. There were pages of MS. on the table and under the table, a batch of typed copy on a chair, single leaves had fluttered away into distant corners; there were there living pages, pages scored and wounded, dead pages that would be burnt at the end of the day—the litter of a cruel battlefield, of a long, long, and desperate fray. Long! I suppose I went to bed sometimes, and got up the same number of times. Yes, I suppose I slept, and ate the food put before me, and talked connectedly to my household on suitable occasions. But I had never been aware of the even flow of daily life, made easy and noiseless for me by a silent, watchful, tireless affection. Indeed, it seemed to me that I had been sitting at that table surrounded by the litter of a desperate fray for days and nights on end. It seemed so, because of the intense weariness of which that interruption had made me aware—the awful disenchantment of a mind realising suddenly the futility of an enormous task, joined to a bodily fatigue such as no ordinary amount of fairly heavy physical labour could ever account for. I have carried bags of wheat on my back, bent almost double under a ship's deck-beams, from six in the morning till six in the evening (with an hour and a half off for meals), so I ought to know.

And I love letters. I am jealous of their honour and concerned for the dignity and comeliness of their service. I was, most likely, the only writer that neat lady had ever caught in the exercise of his craft, and it distressed me not to be able to remember when it was that I dressed myself last, and how. No doubt that would be all right in essentials. The fortune of the house included a pair of grey-blue watchful eyes that would see to that. But I felt somehow as grimy as a Costaguana *lepero* after a day's fighting in the streets, rumpled all over and dishevelled down to my very heels. And I am afraid I blinked stupidly. All this was bad for the honour of letters and the dignity of their service. Seen indistinctly through the dust of my collapsed universe, the good lady glanced about the room with a slightly amused serenity. And she was smiling. What on earth was she smiling at? She remarked casually:

"I am afraid I interrupted you."

"Not at all."

101

She accepted the denial in perfect good faith. And it was strictly true. Interrupted—indeed! She had robbed me of at least twenty lives, each infinitely more poignant and real than her own, because informed with passion, possessed of convictions, involved in great affairs created out of my substance for an anxiously meditated end.

She remained silent for a while, then said with a last glance all round at the litter of the fray:

"And you sit like this here writing your—your . . ."

"I—what? Oh, yes! I sit here all day."

"It must be perfectly delightful."

I suppose that, being no longer very young, I might have been on the verge of having a stroke; but she had left her dog in the porch, and my boy's dog, patrolling the field in front, had espied him from afar. He came on straight and swift like a cannon-ball, and the noise of the fight, which burst suddenly upon our ears, was more than enough to scare away a fit of apoplexy. We went out hastily and separated the gallant animals. Afterwards I told the lady where she would find my wife—just round the corner, under the trees. She nodded and went off with her dog, leaving me appalled before the death and devastation she had lightly made—and with the awfully instructive sound of the word "delightful" lingering in my ears.

Nevertheless, later on, I duly escorted her to the field gate. I wanted to be civil, of course (what are twenty lives in a mere novel that one should be rude to a lady on their account?), but mainly, to adopt the good sound Ollendorffian style, because I did not want the dog of the general's daughter to fight again (*encore*) with the faithful dog of my infant son (*mon petit garçon*). —Was I afraid that the dog of the general's daughter would be able to overcome (*vaincre*) the dog of my child? —No, I was not afraid. . . . But away with the Ollendorff method. However appropriate and seemingly unavoidable when I touch upon anything appertaining to the lady, it is most unsuitable to the origin, character and history of the dog; for the dog was

the gift to the child from a man for whom words had
anything but an Ollendorffian value, a man almost child-
like in the impulsive movements of his untutored genius,
the most single-minded of verbal impressionists, using
his great gifts of straight feeling and right expression with
a fine sincerity and a strong, if, perhaps, not fully conscious conviction. His art did not obtain, I fear, all the
credit its unsophisticated inspiration deserved. I am alluding to the late Stephen Crane, the author of *The Red
Badge of Courage*, a work of imagination which found its
short moment of celebrity in the last decade of the departed century. Other books followed. Not many. He had
not the time. It was an individual and complete talent,
which obtained but a grudging, somewhat supercilious
recognition from the world at large. For himself one hes-
itates to regret his early death. Like one of the men in his
"Open Boat," one felt that he was of those whom fate
seldom allows to make a safe landing after much toil and
bitterness at the oar. I confess to an abiding affection for
that energetic, slight, fragile, intensely living and transient figure. He liked me even before we met on the
strength of a page or two of my writing, and after we had
met I am glad to think he liked me still. He used to point
out to me with great earnestness, and even with some
severity, that "a boy *ought* to have a dog." I suspect that
he was shocked at my neglect of parental duties. Ulti-
mately it was he who provided the dog. Shortly afterwards, one day, after playing with the child on the rug for
an hour or so with the most intense absorption, he raised
his head and declared: "I shall teach your boy to ride."
That was not to be. He was not given the time.

But here is the dog—an old dog now. Broad and low on
his bandy paws, with a black head on a white body, and a
ridiculous black spot at the other end of him, he pro-
vokes, when he walks abroad, smiles not altogether unkind. Grotesque and engaging in the whole of his
appearance, his usual attitudes are meek, but his temper-

ament discloses itself unexpectedly pugnacious in the presence of his kind. As he lies in the firelight, his head well up, and a fixed, far-away gaze directed at the shadows of the room, he achieves a striking nobility of pose in the calm consciousness of an unstained life. He has brought up one baby, and now, after seeing his first charge off to school, he is bringing up another with the same conscientious devotion but with a more deliberate gravity of manner, the sign of greater wisdom and riper experience, but also of rheumatism, I fear. From the morning bath to the evening ceremonies of the cot, you attend the little two-legged creature of your adoption, being yourself treated in the exercise of your duties with every possible regard, with infinite consideration, by every person in the house—even as I myself am treated; only you deserve it more. The general's daughter would tell you that it must be "perfectly delightful."

Aha! old dog. She never heard you yelp with acute pain (it's that poor left ear) the while, with incredible self-command, you preserve a rigid immobility for fear of overturning the little two-legged creature. She has never seen your resigned smile when the little two-legged creature, interrogated sternly, "What are you doing to the good dog?" answers with a wide, innocent stare: "Nothing. Only loving him, mamma dear!"

The general's daughter does not know the secret terms of self-imposed tasks, good dog, the pain that may lurk in the very rewards of rigid self-command. But we have lived together many years. We have grown older, too; and though our work is not quite done yet we may indulge now and then in a little introspection before the fire— meditate on the art of bringing up babies and on the perfect delight of writing tales where so many lives come and go at the cost of one which slips imperceptibly away.

VI

IN the retrospect of a life which had, besides its preliminary stage of childhood and early youth, two distinct
developments, and even two distinct elements, such as
earth and water, for its successive scenes, a certain
amount of naïveness is unavoidable. I am conscious of it
in these pages. This remark is put forward in no apolo-
getic spirit. As years go by and the number of pages grows
steadily, the feeling grows upon one too that one can
write only for friends. Then why should one put them to
the necessity of protesting (as a friend would do) that no
apology is necessary, or put, perchance, into their heads
the doubt of one's discretion? So much as to the care due
to those friends whom a word here, a line there, a fortunate page of just feeling in the right place, some happy
simplicity, or even some lucky subtlety, has drawn from
the great multitude of fellow-beings even as a fish is
drawn from the depths of the sea. Fishing is notoriously (I
am talking now of the deep sea) a matter of luck. As to
one's enemies, those will take care of themselves.

There is a gentleman, for instance, who, metaphori-
cally speaking, jumps upon me with both feet. This image
has no grace, but it is exceedingly apt to the occasion—to
the several occasions. I don't know precisely how long he

105

had been indulging in that intermittent exercise, whose seasons are ruled by the custom of the publishing trade. Somebody pointed him out (in printed shape, of course) to my attention some time ago, and straightway I experienced a sort of reluctant affection for that robust man. He leaves not a shred of my substance untrodden: for the writer's substance is his writing; the rest of him is but a vain shadow, cherished or hated on uncritical grounds. Not a shred! Yet the sentiment owned to is not a freak of affectation or perversity. It has a deeper, and, I venture to think, a more estimable origin than the caprice of emotional lawlessness. It is, indeed, lawful in so much that it is given (reluctantly) for a consideration, for several considerations. There is that robustness, for instance, so often the sign of good moral balance. That's a consideration. It is not, indeed, pleasant to be stamped upon, but the very thoroughness of the operation, implying not only a careful reading, but some real insight into work whose qualities and defects, whatever they may be, are not so much on the surface, is something to be thankful for in view of the fact that it may happen to one's work to be condemned without being read at all. This is the most fatuous adventure that can well happen to a writer venturing his soul among criticisms. It can do one no harm, of course, but it is disagreeable. It is disagreeable in the same way as discovering a three-card-trick man amongst a decent lot of folk in a third-class compartment. The open impudence of the whole transaction, appealing insidiously to the folly and credulity of mankind, the brazen, shameless patter, proclaiming the fraud openly while insisting on the fairness of the game, give one a feeling of sickening disgust. The honest violence of a plain man playing a fair game fairly—even if he means to knock you over—may appear shocking, but it remains within the pale of decency. Damaging as it may be, it is in no sense offensive. One may well feel some regard for honesty, even if practised upon one's own vile body. But it is very obvious that an enemy of that sort will not be stayed by explanations or placated by apologies. Were I to advance the plea of youth in excuse of the naïveness to be found in these pages, he would be likely to say "Bosh!" in a column and a half of fierce print. Yet a writer is no older than his first published book, and, notwithstanding the vain appearances of decay which attend us in this transitory life, I stand here with the wreath of only fifteen short summers on my brow.

With the remark, then, that at such tender age, some naïveness of feeling and expression is excusable, I proceed to admit that, upon the whole, my previous state of existence was not a good equipment for a literary life. Perhaps I should not have used the word literary. That word presupposes an intimacy of acquaintance with letters, a turn of mind and a manner of feeling to which I dare lay no claim. I only love letters; but the love of letters does not make me a literary man, any more than the love of the sea makes a seaman. And it is very possible too, that I love the letters in the same way a literary man may love the sea he looks at from the shore—a scene of great endeavour and of great achievement changing the face of the world, the great open way to all sorts of undiscovered countries. No, perhaps I had better say that the life of the sea—and I don't mean a mere taste of it, but a good broad span of years, something that really counts as real service—is not, upon the whole, a good equipment for a writing life. God forbid, though, that I should be thought of as denying my masters of the quarter-deck. I am not capable of that sort of apostasy. I have confessed my attitude of piety towards their shades in three or four tales, and if any man on earth more than another needs to be true to himself as he hopes to be saved, it is certainly the writer of fiction.

What I mean to say, simply, is that the quarter-deck training does not prepare one sufficiently for the reception of literary criticism. Only that, and no more. But this defect is not without gravity. If it be permissible to twist, invert, adapt (and spoil) M. Anatole France's definition of a good critic, then let us say that the good author is he who contemplates without marked joy or excessive sorrow the adventure of his soul among criticisms. Far be from me the intention to mislead an attentive public into the belief that there is no criticism at sea. That would be dishonest, and even impolite. Everything can be found at sea, according to the spirit of your quest—strife, peace, romance, naturalism of the most pronounced kind, ideals, boredom, disgust, inspiration—and every conceivable opportunity, including the opportunity to make a fool of yourself—exactly as in the pursuit of literature. But the quarter-deck criticism is somewhat different from literary criticism. This much they have in common, that before the one and the other the answering back, as a general rule, does not pay.

Yes, you find criticism at sea, and even appreciation— I tell you everything is to be found on salt water—criticism generally impromptu, and always *viva voce*, which is the outward, obvious difference from the literary operation of that kind, with consequent freshness and vigour which may be lacking in the printed word. With appreciation, which comes at the end, when the critic and the criticised are about to part, it is otherwise. The sea appreciation of one's humble talents has the permanency of the written word, seldom the charm of variety, is formal in its phrasing. There the literary master has the superiority, though he, too, can in effect but say—and often says it in the very phrase—"I can highly recommend." Only usually he uses the word "We," there being some occult virtue in the first person plural, which makes it specially fit for critical and royal declarations. I have a small handful of these sea appreciations, signed by various masters, yellowing slowly in my writing-table's left-hand drawer, rustling under my reverent touch, like a handful of dry leaves plucked for a tender memento from the tree of knowledge. Strange! It seems that it is for these few bits of paper, headed by the names of a few ships and signed by the names of a few Scots and English shipmasters, that I have faced the astonished indignations, the mockeries and the reproaches of a sort hard to bear for a boy of fifteen; that I have been charged with the want of patriotism, the want of sense, and the want of heart too; that I went through agonies of self-conflict and shed secret tears not a few, and had the beauties of the Furca Pass spoiled for me, and have been called an "incorrigible Don Quixote," in allusion to the book-born madness of the knight. For that spoil! They rustle, those bits of paper— some dozen of them in all. In that faint, ghostly sound there live the memories of twenty years, the voices of rough men now no more, the strong voice of the everlasting winds, and the whisper of a mysterious spell, the murmur of the great sea, which must have somehow reached my inland cradle and entered my unconscious ear, like that formula of Mohammedan faith the Mussulman father whispers into the ear of his new-born infant, making him one of the faithful almost with his first breath. I do not know whether I have been a good seaman, but I know I have been a very faithful one. And after all there is that handful of "characters" from various ships to prove that all these years have not been altogether a dream. There they are, brief, and monotonous in tone, but as suggestive bits of writing to me as any inspired page to be found in literature. But then, you see, I have been called romantic. Well, that can't be helped. But stay. I seem to remember that I have been called a realist also. And as that charge too can be made out, let us try to live up to it, at whatever cost, for a change. With this end in view, I will confide to you coyly, and only because there is no one about to see my blushes by the light of the midnight lamp, that these suggestive bits of quarter-deck appreciation one and all contain the words "strictly sober."

Did I overhear a civil murmur, "That's very gratifying, to be sure"? Well, yes, it is gratifying—thank you. It is at least as gratifying to be certified sober as to be certified romantic, though such certificates would not qualify one for the secretaryship of a temperance association or for the post of official troubadour to some lordly democratic institution such as the London County Council, for instance. The above prosaic reflection is put down here only in order to prove the general sobriety of my judgment in mundane affairs. I make a point of it because a couple of years ago, a certain short story of mine being published in a French translation, a Parisian critic—I am almost certain it was M. Gustave Kahn, in the *Gil-Blas*—giving me a short notice, summed up his rapid impression of the writer's quality in the words *un puissant rêveur*. So be it! Who would cavil at the words of a friendly reader? Yet perhaps not such an unconditional dreamer as all that. I will make bold to say that neither at sea nor ashore have I ever lost the sense of responsibility. There is more than one act of intoxication. Even before the most seductive reveries I have remained mindful of that sobriety of interior life, that asceticism of sentiment, in which alone the naked form of truth, such as one conceives it, such as one feels it, can be rendered without shame. It is but a maudlin and indecent verity that comes out through the strength of wine. I have tried to be a sober worker all my life—all my two lives. I did so from taste, no doubt, having an instinctive horror of losing my sense of full self-possession, but also from artistic conviction. Yet there are so many pitfalls on each side of the true path that, having gone some way, and feeling a little battered and weary, as a middle-aged traveller will from the mere daily difficulties of the march, I ask myself whether I have kept always, always faithful to that sobriety wherein there is power, and truth, and peace.

As to my sea-sobriety, that is quite properly certified under the sign-manual of several trustworthy shipmasters of some standing in their time. I seem to hear your polite murmur that "Surely this might have been taken for granted." Well, no. It might not have been. That august academical body of the Marine Department of the Board of Trade takes nothing for granted in the granting of its learned degrees. By its regulations issued under the first Merchant Shipping Act, the very word SOBER must be written, or a whole sackful, a ton, a mountain of the most enthusiastic appreciation will avail you nothing. The door of the examination rooms shall remain closed to your tears and entreaties. The most fanatical advocate of temperance could not be more pitilessly fierce in his rectitude than the Marine Department of the Board of Trade. As I have been face to face at various times with all the examiners of the Port of London, in my generation, there can be no doubt as to the force and the continuity of my abstemiousness. Three of them were examiners in seamanship, and it was my fate to be delivered into the hands of each of them at proper intervals of sea service. The first of all, tall, spare, with a perfectly white head and moustache, a quiet, kindly manner, and an air of benign intelligence, must, I am forced to conclude, have been unfavourably impressed by something in my appearance. His old thin hands loosely clasped resting on his crossed legs, he began by an elementary question in a mild voice, and went on, went on . . . It lasted for hours, for hours. Had I been a strange microbe with potentialities of deadly mischief to the Merchant Service I could not have been submitted to a more miscroscopic examination. Greatly reassured by his apparent benevolence, I had been at first very alert in my answers. But at length the feeling of my brain getting addled crept upon me. And still the passionless process went on, with a sense of untold ages having been spent already on mere preliminaries. Then I got frightened. I was not frightened of being plucked; that eventuality did not present itself to my mind. It was something much more serious, and weird. "This ancient person," I said to myself, terrified, "is so near his grave that he must have lost all notion of time. He is considering this examination in terms of eternity. It is all very well for him. His race is run. But I may find myself coming out of this room into the world of men a stranger, friendless, forgotten by my very landlady, even were I able after this endless experience to remember the way to my hired home." This statement is not so much of a verbal exaggeration as may be supposed. Some very queer thoughts passed through my head while I was considering my answers; thoughts which had nothing to do with seamanship, nor yet with anything reasonable known to this earth. I verily believe that at times I was light-headed in a sort of languid way. At last there fell a silence, and that, too, seemed to last for ages, while, bending over his desk, the examiner wrote out my pass-slip slowly with a noiseless pen. He extended the scrap of paper to me without a word, inclined his white head gravely to my parting bow . . .

When I got out of the room I felt limply flat, like a squeezed lemon, and the doorkeeper in his glass cage, where I stopped to get my hat and tip him a shilling, said:

"Well! I thought you were never coming out."

"How long have I been in there?" I asked faintly.

He pulled out his watch.

"He kept you, sir, just under three hours. I don't think this ever happened with any of the gentlemen before."

It was only when I got out of the building that I began to walk on air. And the human animal being averse from change and timid before the unknown, I said to myself that I would not mind really being examined by the same man on a future occasion. But when the time of ordeal came round again the doorkeeper let me into another room, with the now familiar paraphernalia of models of ships and tackle, a board for signals on the wall, a big long table covered with official forms, and having an unrigged mast fixed to the edge. The solitary tenant was unknown to me by sight, though not by reputation, which was simply execrable. Short and sturdy as far as I could judge, clad in an old brown morning-suit, he sat leaning on his elbow, his hand shading his eyes, and half averted from the chair I was to occupy on the other side of the table. He was motionless, mysterious, remote, enigmatical, with something mournful too in the pose, like that statue of Giuliano (I think) de Medici shading his face on the tomb by Michael Angelo, though, of course, he was far, far from being beautiful. He began by trying to make me talk nonsense. But I had been warned of that fiendish trait, and contradicted him with great assurance. After a while he left off. So far, good. But his immobility, the thick elbow on the table, the abrupt, unhappy voice, the shaded and averted face grew more and more impressive. He kept inscrutably silent for a moment, and then, placing me in a ship of a certain size at sea, under certain conditions of weather, season, locality, etc., etc.—all very clear and precise—ordered me to execute a certain manœuvre. Before I was half through with it he did some material damage to the ship. Directly I had grappled with the difficulty he caused another to present itself, and when that too was met he stuck another ship before me, creating a very dangerous situation. I felt slightly outraged by this ingenuity in piling up trouble upon a man.

"I wouldn't have got into that mess," I suggested mildly. "I could have seen that ship before."

He never stirred the least bit.

"No, you couldn't. The weather's thick."

"Oh! I didn't know," I apologised, blankly. I suppose that after all I managed to stave off the smash with sufficient approach to verismilitude, and the ghastly business went on. You must understand that the scheme of the test he was applying to me was, I gathered, a homeward passage—the sort of passage I would not wish to my bitterest enemy. That imaginary ship seemed to labour

113

under a most comprehensive curse. It's no use enlarging on these never-ending misfortunes; suffice it to say that long before the end I would have welcomed with gratitide an opportunity to exchange into the *Flying Dutchman*. Finally he shoved me into the North Sea (I suppose) and provided me with a lee shore with outlying sandbanks— the Dutch coast presumably. Distance, eight miles. The evidence of such implacable animosity deprived me of speech for quite half a minute.

"Well," he said—for our pace had been very smart indeed till then.

"I will have to think a little, sir."

"Doesn't look as if there were much time to think," he muttered, sardonically, from under his hand.

"No, sir," I said with some warmth. "Not on board a ship I could see. But so many accidents have happened that I really can't remember what there's left for me to work with."

Still half averted, and with his eyes concealed, he made unexpectedly a grunting remark.

"You've done very well."

"Have I the two anchors at the bow, sir?" I asked.

"Yes."

I prepared myself then, as a last hope for the ship, to let them both go in the most effectual manner, when his infernal system of testing resourcefulness came into play again.

"But there's only one cable. You've lost the other."

It was exasperating.

"Then I would back them, if I could, and tail the heaviest hawser on board on the end of the chain before letting go, and if she parted from that, which is quite likely, I would just do nothing. She would have to go."

"Nothing more to do, eh?"

"No, sir. I could do no more."

He gave a bitter half-laugh.

"You could always say your prayers."

114

He got up, stretched himself, and yawned slightly. It was a sallow, strong, unamiable face. He put me, in a surly, bored fashion, through the usual questions as to lights and signals, and I escaped from the room thankfully—passed! Forty minutes! And again I walked on air along Tower Hill, where so many good men had lost their heads, because, I suppose, they were not re-sourceful enough to save them. And in my heart of hearts I had no objection to meeting that examiner once more when the third and last ordeal became due in another year or so. I even hoped I should. I knew the worst of him now, and forty minutes is not an unreasonable time. Yes, I distinctly hoped . . .

But not a bit of it. When I presented myself to be ex-amined for Master the examiner who received me was short, plump, with a round, soft face in grey, fluffy whis-kers, and fresh, loquacious lips.

He commenced operations with an easy-going "Let's see. H'm. Suppose you tell me all you know of char-ter-parties." He kept it up in that style all through, wan-dering off in the shape of comment into bits out of his own life, then pulling himself up short and returning to the business in hand. It was very interesting. "What's your idea of a jury-rudder now?" he queried suddenly, at the end of an instructive anecdote bearing upon a point of stowage.

I warned him that I had no experience of a lost rudder at sea, and gave him two classical examples of makeshifts out of a text-book. In exchange he described to me a jury-rudder he had invented himself years before, when in command of a three-thousand-ton steamer. It was, I de-clare, the cleverest contrivance imaginable. "May be of use to you some day," he concluded. "You will go into steam presently. Everybody goes into steam."

There he was wrong. I never went into steam—not really. If I only live long enough I shall become a bizarre relic of a dead barbarism, a sort of monstrous antiquity, the only seaman of the dark ages who had never gone into steam—not really.

Before the examination was over he imparted to me a few interesting details of the transport service in the time of the Crimean War.

"The use of wire rigging became general about that time, too," he observed. "I was a very young master then. That was before you were born."

"Yes, sir. I am of the year 1857."

"The Mutiny year," he commented, as if to himself, adding in a louder tone that his ship happened then to be in the Gulf of Bengal, employed under a government charter.

Clearly the transport service had been the making of this examiner, who so unexpectedly had given me an insight into his existence, awakening in me the sense of the continuity of that sea life into which I had stepped from outside; giving a touch of human intimacy to the machinery of official relations. I felt adopted. His experience was for me, too, as though he had been an ancestor.

Writing my long name (it has twelve letters) with laborious care on the slip of blue paper, he remarked:

"You are of Polish extraction."

"Born there, sir."

He laid down the pen and leaned back to look at me as if it were for the first time.

"Not many of your nationality in our service, I should think. I never remember meeting one either before or after I left the sea. Don't remember ever hearing of one. An inland people, aren't you?"

I said yes—very much so. We were remote from the sea not only by situation, but also from a complete absence of indirect association, not being a commercial nation at all, but purely agricultural. He made then the quaint reflection that it was "a long way for me to come out to begin a sea life"; as if sea life were not precisely a life in which one goes a long way from home.

116

I told him, smiling, that no doubt I could have found a ship much nearer to my native place, but I had thought to myself that if I was to be a seaman, then I would be a British seaman and no other. It was a matter of deliberate choice.

He nodded slightly at that; and as he kept on looking at me interrogatively, I enlarged a little, confessing that I had spent a little time on the way in the Mediterranean and in the West Indies. I did not want to present myself to the British Merchant Service in an altogether green state. It was no use telling him that my mysterious vocation was so strong that my very wild oats had to be sown at sea. It was the exact truth, but he would not have understood the somewhat exceptional psychology of my sea-going, I fear.

"I suppose you've never come across one of your countrymen at sea. Have you, now?"

I admitted I never had. The examiner had given himself up to the spirit of gossiping idleness. For myself, I was in no haste to leave that room. Not in the least. The era of examinations was over. I would never again see that friendly man who was a professional ancestor, a sort of grandfather in the craft. Moreover, I had to wait till he dismissed me, and of that there was no sign. As he remained silent, looking at me, I added:

"But I have heard of one, some years ago. He seems to have been a boy serving his time on board a Liverpool ship, if I am not mistaken."

"What was his name?"

I told him.

"How did you say that?" he asked, puckering up his eyes at the uncouth sound.

I repeated the name very distinctly.

"How do you spell it?"

I told him. He moved his head at the impracticable nature of that name, and observed:

"It's quite as long as your own—isn't it?"

There was no hurry. I had passed for Master, and I had all the rest of my life before me to make the best of it. That seemed a long time. I went leisurely through a small mental calculation, and said:

"Not quite. Shorter by two letters, sir."

"Is it?" The examiner pushed the signed blue slip across the table to me, and rose from his chair. Somehow this seemed a very abrupt ending of our relations, and I felt almost sorry to part from that excellent man, who was master of a ship before the whisper of the sea had reached my cradle. He offered me his hand and wished me well. He even made a few steps toward the door with me, and ended with good-natured advice.

"I don't know what may be your plans, but you ought to go into steam. When a man has got his master's certificate it's the proper time. If I were you I would go into steam."

I thanked him, and shut the door behind me definitely on the era of examinations. But that time I did not walk on air, as on the first two occasions. I walked across the Hill of many beheadings with measured steps. It was a fact, I said to myself, that I was now a British master mariner beyond a doubt. It was not that I had an exaggerated sense of that very modest achievement, with which, however, luck, opportunity, or any extraneous influence could have had nothing to do. That fact, satisfactory and obscure in itself, had for me a certain ideal significance. It was an answer to certain outspoken scepticism and even to some not very kind aspersions. I had vindicated myself from what had been cried upon as a stupid obstinacy or a fantastic caprice. I don't mean to say that a whole country had been convulsed by my desire to go to sea. But for a boy between fifteen and sixteen, sensitive enough, in all conscience, the commotion of his little world had seemed a very considerable thing indeed. So considerable that, absurdly enough, the echoes of it linger to this day. I catch myself in hours of solitude and retrospect meeting arguments and charges made thirty-five years ago by voices now forever still; finding things to say that an assailed boy could not have found, simply because of the mysteriousness of his impulses to himself. I understood no more than the people who called upon me to explain myself. There was no precedent. I verily believe mine was the only case of a boy of my nationality and my antecedents taking a, so to speak, standing jump out of his racial surroundings and associations. For you must understand that there was no idea of any sort of "career" in my call. Of Russia or Germany there could be no question. The nationality, the antecedents, made it impossible. The feeling against the Austrian service was not so strong, and I dare say there would have been no difficulty in finding my way into the Naval School at Pola. It would have meant six months' extra grinding at German, perhaps, but I was not past the age of admission, and in other respects I was well qualified. This expedient to palliate my folly was thought of—but not by me. I must admit that in that respect my negative was accepted at once. That order of feeling was comprehensible enough to the most inimical of my critics. I was not called upon to offer explanations; the truth is that what I had in view was not a naval career, but the sea. There seemed no way open to it but through France. I had the language at any rate, and of all the countries in Europe it is with France that Poland has most connection. There were some facilities for having me a little looked after, at first. Letters were being written, answers were being received, arrangements were being made for my departure for Marseilles, where an excellent fellow called Solary, got at in a roundabout fashion through various French channels, had promised good-naturedly to put *le jeune homme* in the way of getting a decent ship for his first start if he really wanted a taste of *ce métier de chien*.

I watched all these preparations gratefully, and kept my own counsel. But what I told the last of my examiners was perfectly true. Already the determined resolve, that "if a seaman, then an English seaman," was formulated in my head though, of course, in the Polish language. I did not know six words of English, and I was astute enough to understand that it was much better to say nothing of my purpose. As it was I was already looked upon as partly insane, at least by the more distant acquaintances. The principal thing was to get away. I put my trust in the good-natured Solary's very civil letter to my uncle, though I was shocked a little by the phrase about the *métier de chien*.

This Solary (Baptistin), when I beheld him, in the flesh, turned out a quite young man, very good-looking, with a fine black, short beard, a fresh complexion, and soft, merry black eyes. He was as jovial and good-natured as any boy could desire. I was still asleep in my room in a modest hotel near the quays of the old port, after the fatigues of the journey *via* Vienna, Zurich, Lyons, when he burst in, flinging the shutters open to the sun of Provence and chiding me boisterously for lying abed. How pleasantly he startled me by his noisy objurgations to be up and off instantly for a "three years' campaign in the South Seas." O magic words! *"Une campagne de trois ans dans les mers du sud"*—that is the French for a three years' deep-water voyage.

He gave me a delightful waking, and his friendliness was unwearied; but I fear he did not enter upon a quest for a ship for me in a very solemn spirit. He had been at sea himself, but had left off at the age of twenty-five, finding he could earn his living on shore in a much more agreeable manner. He was related to an incredible number of Marseilles well-to-do families of a certain class. One of his uncles was a ship-broker of good standing, with a large connection amongst English ships; other relatives of his dealt in ships' stores, owned sail-lofts, sold chains and anchors, were master-stevedores, caulkers, shipwrights. His grandfather (I think) was a dignitary of a kind, the

Syndic of the Pilots. I made acquaintances amongst these people, but mainly amongst the pilots. The very first whole day I ever spent on salt water was by invitation, in a big half-decked pilot-boat, cruising under close reefs on the lookout, in misty, blowing weather, for the sails of ships and the smoke of steamers rising out there, beyond the slim and tall Planier lighthouse cutting the line of the wind-swept horizon with a white perpendicular stroke. They were hospitable souls, these sturdy Provençal sea-men. Under the general designation of *le petit ami de Baptistin* I was made the guest of the Corporation of Pilots, and had the freedom of their boats night or day. And many a day and a night too did I spend cruising with these rough, kindly men, under whose auspices my intimacy with the sea began. Many a time "the little friend of Baptistin" had the hooded cloak of the Mediterranean sailor thrown over him by their honest hands while dodging at night under the lee of Château d'If on the watch for the lights of ships. Their sea-tanned faces, whiskered or shaved, lean or full, with the intent wrinkled sea eyes of the pilot breed, and here and there a thin gold loop at the lobe of a hairy ear, bent over my sea infancy. The first operation of seamanship I had an opportunity of observing was the boarding of ships at sea, at all times, in all states of the weather. They gave it to me to the full. And I have been invited to sit in more than one tall, dark house of the old town at their hospitable board, had the *bouillabaisse* ladled out into a thick plate by their high-voiced, broad-browed wives, talked to their daughters— thick-set girls, with pure profiles, glorious masses of black hair arranged with complicated art, dark eyes, and dazzlingly white teeth.

I had also other acquaintances of quite a different sort. One of them, Madame Delestang, an imperious, handsome lady in a statuesque style, would carry me off now and then on the front seat of her carriage to the Prado, at the hour of fashionable airing. She belonged to one of the old aristocratic families in the south. In her haughty weariness she used to make me think of Lady Dedlock in Dickens' *Bleak House,* a work of the master for which I have such an admiration, or rather such an intense and unreasoning affection, dating from the days of my childhood, that its very weaknesses are more precious to me than the strength of other men's work. I have read it innumerable times, both in Polish and in English; I have read it only the other day, and, by a not very surprising inversion, the Lady Dedlock of the book reminded me strongly of the *belle Madame Delestang.*

Her husband (as I sat facing them both), with his thin bony nose, and a perfectly bloodless, narrow physiognomy clamped together as it were by short formal side-whiskers, had nothing of Sir Leicester Dedlock's "grand air" and courtly solemnity. He belonged to the *haute bourgeoisie* only, and was a banker, with whom a modest credit had been opened for my needs. He was such an ardent—no, such a frozen-up, mummified Royalist that he used in current conversation turns of speech contemporary, I should say, with the good Henri Quatre; and when talking of money matters reckoned not in francs, like the common, godless herd of post-Revolutionary Frenchmen, but in obsolete and forgotten *écus—écus* of all money units in the world!—as though Louis Quatorze were still promenading in royal splendour the gardens of Versailles, and Monsieur de Colbert busy with the direction of maritime affairs. You must admit that in a banker of the nineteenth century it was a quaint idiosyncrasy. Luckily in the counting-house (it occupied part of the ground floor of the Delestang town residence, in a silent, shady street) the accounts were kept in modern money so that I never had any difficulty in making my wants known to the grave, low-voiced, decorous, Legitimist (I suppose) clerks, sitting in the perpetual gloom of heavily-barred windows behind the sombre, ancient counters, beneath lofty ceilings with heavily-moulded cornices. I always felt on going out as though I had been in the temple of some dignified but completely temporal religion. And it was generally on these occasions that under the great carriage gateway Lady Ded—I mean Madame Delestang, catching sight of my raised hat, would beckon me with an amiable imperiousness to the side of the carriage, and suggest with an air of amused nonchalance, *"Venez donc faire un tour avec nous,"* to which the husband would add an encouraging *"C'est ça. Allons, montez, jeune homme."* He questioned me sometimes, significantly but with perfect tact and delicacy, as to the way I employed my time, and never failed to express the hope that I wrote regularly to my "honoured uncle." I made no secret of the way I employed my time, and I rather fancy that my artless tales of the pilots and so on entertained Madame Delestang, so far as that ineffable woman could be entertained by the prattle of a youngster very full of his new experience amongst strange men and strange sensations. She expressed no opinions, and talked to me very little; yet her portrait hangs in the gallery of my intimate memories, fixed there by a short and fleeting episode. One day, after putting me down at the corner of a street, she offered me her hand, and detained me by a slight pressure, for a moment. While the husband sat motionless and looking straight before him, she leaned forward in the carriage to say, with just a shade of warning in her leisurely tone: *"Il faut, cependant, faire attention à ne pas gâter sa vie."* I had never seen her face so close to mine before. She made my heart beat, and caused me to remain thoughtful for a whole evening. Certainly one must, after all, take care not to spoil one's life. But she did not know—nobody could know—how impossible that danger seemed to me.

123

VII

CAN the transports of first love be calmed, checked, turned to a cold suspicion of the future by a grave quotation from a work on Political Economy? I ask—Is it conceivable? Is it possible? Would it be right? With my feet on the very shores of the sea and about to embrace my blue-eyed dream, what could a good-natured warning as to spoiling one's life mean to my youthful passion? It was the most unexpected and the last, too, of the many warnings I had received. It sounded to me very *bizarre*— and, uttered as it was in the very presence of my enchantress, like the voice of folly, the voice of ignorance. But I was not so callous or so stupid as not to recognise there also the voice of kindness. And then the vagueness of the warning—because what can be the meaning of the phrase: to spoil one's life?—arrested one's attention by its air of wise profundity. At any rate, as I have said before, the words of *la belle Madame Delestang* made me thoughtful for a whole evening. I tried to understand and tried in vain, not having any notion of life as an enterprise that could be mismanaged. But I left off being thoughtful; shortly before midnight, at which hour, haunted by no ghosts of the past and by no visions of the future, I walked down the quay of the *Vieux Port* to join the pilot-boat of

125

my friends. I knew where she would be waiting for her crew, in the little bit of a canal behind the Fort at the entrance of the harbour. The deserted quays looked very white and dry in the moonlight and as if frost-bound in the sharp air of that December night. A prowler or two slunk by noiselessly; a custom-house guard, soldier-like, a sword by his side, paced close under the bowsprits of the long row of ships moored bows on opposite the long, slightly curved, continuous flat wall of the tall houses that seemed to be one immense abandoned building with innumerable windows shuttered closely. Only here and there a small, dingy *café* for sailors cast a yellow gleam on the bluish sheen of the flagstone. Passing by, one heard a deep murmur of voices inside—nothing more. How quiet everything was at the end of the quays on the last night on which I went out for a service cruise as a guest of the Marseilles pilots! Not a footstep, except my own, not a sigh, not a whispering echo of the usual revelry going on in the narrow, unspeakable lanes of the Old Town reached my ear—and suddenly, with a terrific jingling rattle of iron and glass, the omnibus of the Jolliette on its last journey swung round the corner of the dead wall which faces across the paved road the characteristic angular mass of the Fort St. Jean. Three horses trotted abreast with the clatter of hoofs on the granite setts, and the yellow, uproarious machine jolted violently behind them, fantastic, lighted up, perfectly empty and with the driver apparently asleep on his swaying perch above that amazing racket. I flattened myself against the wall and gasped. It was a stunning experience. Then after staggering on a few paces in the shadow of the Fort casting a darkness more intense than that of a clouded night upon the canal, I saw the tiny light of a lantern standing on the quay, and became aware of muffled figures making towards it from various directions—Pilots of the Third Company hastening to embark. Too sleepy to be talkative, they step on board in silence. But a few low grunts and an enormous yawn are heard. Somebody even ejaculates: *"Ah! Coquin de sort!"* and sighs wearily at his hard fate.

The *patron* of the Third Company (there were five companies of pilots at that time, I believe) is the brother-in-law of my friend Solary (Baptistin), a broad-shouldered, deep-chested man of forty, with a keen, frank glance which always seeks your eyes. He greets me by a low, hearty *"Hé, l'ami. Comment va?"* With his clipped moustache and massive open face, energetic and at the same time placid in expression, he is a fine specimen of the southerner of the calm type. For there is such a type in which the volatile southern passion is transmuted into solid force. He is fair, but no one could mistake him for a man of the north even by the dim gleam of the lantern standing on the quay. He is worth a dozen of your ordinary Normans or Bretons, but then, in the whole immense sweep of the Mediterranean shores, you could not find half a dozen men of his stamp.

Standing by the tiller, he pulls out his watch from under a thick jacket and bends his head over it in the light cast into the boat. Time's up. His pleasant voice commands in a quiet undertone, *"Larguez."* A suddenly projected arm snatches the lantern off the quay—and, warped along by a line at first, then with the regular tug of four heavy sweeps in the bow, the big half-decked boat full of men glides out of the black, breathless shadow of the Fort. The open water of the *avant-port* glitters under the moon as if sown over with millions of sequins, and the long white breakwater shines like a thick bar of solid silver. With a quick rattle of blocks and one single silky swish, the sail is filled by a little breeze keen enough to have come straight down from the frozen moon, and the boat, after the clatter of the hauled-in sweeps, seems to stand at rest, surrounded by a mysterious whispering so faint and unearthly that it may be the rustling of the brilliant, overpowering moonrays breaking like a rain-shower upon the hard, smooth, shadowless sea.

I may well remember that last night spent with the pilots of the Third Company. I have known the spell of moonlight since, on various seas and coasts—coasts of forests, of rocks, of sand dunes—but no magic so perfect in its revelation of unsuspected character, as though one were allowed to look upon the mystic nature of material things. For hours I suppose no word was spoken in that boat. The pilots seated in two rows facing each other dozed with their arms folded and their chins resting upon their breasts. They displayed a great variety of caps: cloth, wool, leather, ear-flaps, tassels, with a picturesque round *béret* or two down over the brows; and one grandfather, with a shaved, bony face and a great beak of a nose, had a cloak with a hood which made him look in our midst like a cowled monk being carried off goodness knows where by that silent company of seamen—quiet enough to be dead.

My fingers itched for the tiller, and in due course my friend, the *patron*, surrendered it to me in the same spirit in which the family coachman lets a boy hold the reins on an easy bit of road. There was a great solitude around us; the islets ahead, Monte Cristo and the Château d'If in full light, seemed to float toward us—so steady, so imperceptible was the progress of our boat. "Keep her in the furrow of the moon," the *patron* directed me in a quiet murmur, sitting down ponderously in the stern-sheets and reaching for his pipe.

The pilot station in weather like this was only a mile or two to the westward of the islets; and presently, as we approached the spot, the boat we were going to relieve swam into our view suddenly, on her way home, cutting black and sinister into the wake of the moon under a sable wing, while to them our sail must have been a vision of white and dazzling radiance. Without altering the course a hair's-breadth, we slipped by each other within an oar's-length. A drawling sardonic hail came out of her. Instantly, as if by magic, our dozing pilots got on their feet in a body. An incredible babel of bantering shouts burst out, a jocular, passionate, voluble chatter, which lasted till the boats were stern to stern, theirs all bright now and with a shining sail to our eye, we turned all black to their vision, and drawing away from them under a sable wing. That extraordinary uproar died away almost as suddenly as it had begun; first one had enough of it and sat down, then another, then three or four together, and when all had left off with mutters and growling half-laughs the sound of hearty chuckling became audible, persistent, unnoticed. The cowled grandfather was very much entertained somewhere within his hood.

He had not joined in the shouting of jokes, neither had he moved the least bit. He had remained quietly in his place against the foot of the mast. I had been given to understand long before that he had the rating of a second-class able seaman (*matelot léger*) in the fleet which sailed from Toulon for the conquest of Algeria in the year of grace 1830. And, indeed, I had seen and examined one of the buttons of his old brown patched coat, the only brass button of the miscellaneous lot, flat and thin, with the words *Équipages de ligne* engraved on it. That sort of button, I believe, went out with the last of the French Bourbons. "I preserved it from the time of my Navy Service," he explained, nodding rapidly his frail, vulture-like head. It was not very likely that he had picked up that relic in the street. He looked certainly old enough to have fought at Trafalgar—or at any rate to have played his little part there as a powder-monkey. Shortly after we had been introduced he had informed me in a Franco-Provençal jargon, that when he was a "shaver no higher than that" he had seen the Emperor Napoleon returning from Elba. It was at night, he narrated vaguely, without animation, at a spot between Fréjus and Antibes in the open country. A big fire had been lit at the side of the cross-roads. The population from several villages had collected there, old and young—down to the very children in arms because the women had refused to stay at home. Tall soldiers, wearing high, hairy caps, stood in a circle facing the people silently, and their stern eyes and big moustaches were enough to make everybody keep at a distance. He, "being an impudent little shaver," wriggled out of the crowd, creeping on his hands and knees as near as he dared to the grenadiers' legs, and peeping through discovered, standing perfectly still in the light of the fire, "a little fat fellow in a three-cornered hat, buttoned up in a long straight coat, with a big, pale face inclined on one shoulder, looking something like a priest. His hands were clasped behind his back . . . It appears that this was the Emperor," the Ancient commented with a faint sigh. He was staring from the ground with all his might, when "my poor father," who had been searching for his boy frantically everywhere, pounced upon him and hauled him away by the ear.

The tale seems an authentic recollection. He related it to me many times, using the very same words. The grandfather honoured me by a special and somewhat embarrassing predilection. Extremes touch. He was the oldest member by a long way in that Company, and I was, if I may say so, its temporarily adopted baby. He had been a pilot longer than any man in the boat could remember; thirty—forty years. He did not seem certain himself, but it could be found out, he suggested, in the archives of the Pilot Office. He had been pensioned off years before, but he went out from force of habit; and, as my friend the *patron* of the Company once confided to me in a whisper, "the old chap did no harm. He was not in the way." They treated him with rough deference. One and another would address some insignificant remark to him now and again, but nobody really took any notice of what he had to say. He had survived his strength, his usefulness, his very wisdom. He wore long, green, worsted stockings, pulled up above the knee over his trousers, a sort of woollen nightcap on his hairless cranium, and wooden clogs on his feet. Without his hooded cloak he looked like a peasant. Half a dozen hands would be extended to help him on board, but afterwards he was left pretty much to his own thoughts. Of course he never did any work, except, perhaps, to cast off some rope when hailed: *"Hé, l'Ancien!* let go the halyards there, at your hand"—or some such request of an easy kind.

No one took notice in any way of the chuckling within the shadow of the hood. He kept it up for a long time with intense enjoyment. Obviously he had preserved intact the innocence of mind which is easily amused. But when his hilarity had exhausted itself, he made a professional remark in a self-assertive but quavering voice:

"Can't expect much work on a night like this."

No one took it up. It was a mere truism. Nothing under canvas could be expected to make a port on such an idle night of dreamy splendour and spiritual stillness. We would have to glide idly to and fro, keeping our station within the appointed bearings, and, unless a fresh breeze sprang up with the dawn, we would land before sunrise on a small islet that, within two miles of us, shone like a lump of frozen moonlight, to "break a crust and take a pull at the wine bottle." I was familiar with the procedure. The stout boat emptied of her crowd would nestle her buoyant, capable side against the very rock—such is the perfectly smooth amenity of the classic sea when in a gentle mood. The crust broken, and the mouthful of wine swallowed—it was literally no more than that with this abstemious race—the pilots would pass the time stamping their feet on the slabs of sea-salted stone and blowing into their nipped fingers. One or two misanthropists would sit apart perched on boulders like manlike sea-fowl of solitary habits; the sociably disposed would gossip scandalously in little gesticulating knots; and there would be perpetually one or another of my hosts taking aim at the empty horizon with the long, brass tube of the telescope, a heavy, murderous-looking piece of collective property, everlastingly changing hands with brandishing and levelling movements. Then about noon (it was a short turn of duty—the long turn lasted twenty-four hours) another boatful of pilots would relieve us—and we should steer for the old Phœnician port, dominated, watched over from the ridge of a dust-grey, arid hill by the red-and-white-striped pile of the Notre Dame de la Garde.

All this came to pass as I had foreseen in the fullness of my very recent experience. But also something not foreseen by me did happen, something which causes me to remember my last outing with the pilots. It was on this occasion that my hand touched, for the first time, the side of an English ship.

No fresh breeze had come with the dawn, only the steady little draught got a more keen edge on it as the eastern sky became bright and glassy with a clean, colourless light. It was while we were all ashore on the islet that a steamer was picked up by the telescope, a black speck like an insect posed on the hard edge of the offing. She emerged rapidly to her water-line and came on steadily, a slim hull with a long streak of smoke slanting away from the rising sun. We embarked in a hurry, and headed the boat out for our prey, but we hardly moved three miles an hour.

She was a big, high-class cargo-steamer of a type that is to be met on the sea no more—black hull, with low, white superstructures, powerfully rigged with three masts and a lot of yards on the fore; two hands at her enormous wheel—steam steering-gear was not a matter of course in these days—and with them on the bridge three others, bulky in thick blue jackets, ruddy-faced, muffled up, with peaked caps—I suppose all her officers. There are ships I have met more than once and known well by sight whose names I have forgotten; but the name of that ship seen once so many years ago in the clear flush of a cold pale sunrise I have not forgotten. How could I—the first English ship on whose side I ever laid my hand! The name—

I read it letter by letter on the bow—was *James Westoll*. Not very romantic you will say. The name of a very considerable, well-known and universally respected North-country ship-owner, I believe. James Westoll! What better name could an honourable hard-working ship have? To me the very grouping of the letters is alive with the romantic feeling of her reality as I saw her floating motionless and borrowing an ideal grace from the austere purity of the light.

We were then very near her and, on a sudden impulse, I volunteered to pull bow in the dinghy which shoved off at once to put the pilot on board while our boat, fanned by the faint air which had attended us all through the night, went on gliding gently past the black glistening length of the ship. A few strokes brought us alongside, and it was then that, for the very first time in my life, I heard myself addressed in English—the speech of my secret choice, of my future, of long friendships, of the deepest affections, of hours of toil and hours of ease, and of solitary hours too, of books read, of thoughts pursued, of remembered emotions—of my very dreams! And if (after being thus fashioned by it in that part of me which cannot decay) I dare not claim it aloud as my own, then, at any rate, the speech of my children. Thus small events grow memorable by the passage of time. As to the quality of the address itself I cannot say it was very striking. Too short for eloquence and devoid of all charm of tone, it consisted precisely of the three words "Look out there!" growled out huskily above my head.

It proceeded from a big fat fellow (he had an obtrusive, hairy double chin) in a blue woollen shirt and roomy breeches pulled up very high, even to the level of his breast-bone, by a pair of braces quite exposed to public view. As where he stood there was no bulwark, but only a rail and stanchions, I was able to take in at a glance the whole of his voluminous person from his feet to the high crown of his soft black hat, which sat like an absurd flanged cone on his big head. The grotesque and massive aspect of that deck-hand (I suppose he was that—very likely the lamp-trimmer) surprised me very much. My course of reading, of dreaming and longing for the sea had not prepared me for a sea brother of that sort. I never met again a figure in the least like his except in the illustrations to Mr. W. W. Jacobs' most entertaining tales of barges and coasters; but the inspired talent of Mr. Jacobs for poking endless fun at poor, innocent sailors in a prose which, however extravagant in its felicitous invention, is always artistically adjusted to observed truth, was not yet. Perhaps Mr. Jacobs himself was not yet. I fancy that, at most, if he had made his nurse laugh it was about all he had achieved at that early date.

Therefore, I repeat, other disabilities apart, I could not have been prepared for the sight of that husky old porpoise. The object of his concise address was to call my attention to a rope which he incontinently flung down for me to catch. I caught it, though it was not really necessary, the ship having no way on her by that time. Then everything went on very swiftly. The dinghy came with a slight bump against the steamer's side, the pilot, grabbing the rope ladder, had scrambled half-way up before I knew that our task of boarding was done; the harsh, muffled clanging of the engine-room telegraph struck my ear through the iron plate; my companion in the dinghy was urging me to "shove off—push hard"; and when I bore against the smooth flank of the first English ship I ever touched in my life, I felt it already throbbing under my open palm.

Her head swung a little to the west, pointing towards the miniature lighthouse of the Jolliette breakwater, far away there, hardly distinguishable against the land. The dinghy danced a squashy, splashy jig in the wash of the wake and turning in my seat I followed the *James Westoll* with my eyes. Before she had gone in a quarter of a mile she hoisted her flag, as the harbour regulations prescribe for arriving and departing ships. I saw it suddenly flicker and stream out on the flagstaff. The Red Ensign! In the pellucid, colourless atmosphere bathing the drab and grey masses of that southern land, the livid islets, the sea of pale glassy blue under the pale glassy sky of that cold sunrise, it was, as far as the eye could reach, the only spot of ardent colour—flame-like, intense, and presently as minute as the tiny red spark the concentrated reflection of a great fire kindles in the clear heart of a globe of crystal. The Red Ensign—the symbolic, protecting, warm bit of bunting flung wide upon the seas, and destined for so many years to be the only roof over my head.

THE END

AFTERWORD

A S A a writer I could wish I had been endowed with Dostoevsky's diabolic insight into the unconscious, or Dickens's grotesque inventiveness, or Faulkner's uninhibited verbal power. But it is rather the prose rhythms and impressionist novel structures of Conrad with which I feel the closest affinity, and he is certainly the writer who has had the greatest influence on my fiction. So it was only inevitable that my own wandering autobiographical volume of 1980, *The Touch of Time: Myth, Memory and the Self*, should reflect an unconscious allegiance to the second of Conrad's autobiographies, *A Personal Record* (1912).

In *The Mirror of the Sea* (1906) the Conrad perhaps suffering from a *crise de quarante*, among many other neurotic ailments, reinvented a romantic period of his youth so plausibly that it was long accepted by biographers as fact: the romantic suggestion of an affair with the mistress of a royal personage, a duel fought in consequence. It is even possible that Conrad himself at times believed that the wound near his heart came from a duel rather than attempted suicide, just as Faulkner at times may have convinced himself that he had actually been wounded in the war. An inventive writer's capacity to believe his own inventions, and to give his fantasies the finest tones of reality, can hardly be overemphasized. My own childhood acquaintaince with the Hungarian actress Lya de Putti, which lasted only a few days, eventually became a deliberately cherished personal myth reflected in no less than three of my novels. I even feel a fraternal bond with the Dickens whose reveries led him to believe he was in love with the young Queen Victoria. In reinventing the world, and in saying his reinvention is truer than "real reality," the novelist is only following his vocation. In his great autobiography *Si le grain ne meurt* (in English *If It Die*) André Gide expressed with scrupulous sincerity not the flesh and blood person his friends knew, but a meaningful created persona and essential self-image. Art purifies history by rewriting it.

The Conrad of *A Personal Record* does not, so far as I know, seriously alter fact, and one of his central themes is Fidelity, a word he liked to capitalize: fidelity to the Poland he had been accused of abandoning, fidelity to the aristocratic ideal of *noblesse oblige* and sympathy for the underprivileged of the earth, fidelity to professional obligations as seaman and writer, fidelity to his own youthful ideal of self, and, not least, fidelity to a "sobriety of interior life, that asceticism of sentiment, in which alone the naked form of truth, such as one conceives it, such as one feels it, can be rendered without shame." In returning to crucial moments of his earlier life, and in wanting to establish a vital personal connection between *then* and *now*, Conrad shares the aims of Proust and Gide, of Wordsworth in *The Prelude*, of Rousseau in his *Confessions* and perhaps St. Augustine in his, of Dickens in *The Uncommercial Traveler*, of Mark Twain in parts of *Life on the Mississippi*, of Nabokov in *Speak, Memory*, and (altogether worthy to belong in this august company) of my father in his *Personal Equation*.

These works have in common three modes that cause them to differ from most autobiographies.

First, they select and vivify certain remembered moments (it may be Rousseau's stolen ribbon or Wordsorth's solitary ice-skating or Conrad's sight of an oddly dressed Englishman on the Furka Pass) while omitting much more obvious ones—as though to remind us how large in our lives the small, the casual and the unexpected may eventually loom;

Second, they eschew chronology to wander freely in time, proceeding by conceptual or even verbal association from past to present and present to past. The freedom is, of course, an exquisitely controlled freedom. In this *A Personal Record* pursues the methods of the impressionist novel perfected in *Lord Jim* twelve years before. The true reality of our interior lives does, after all, escape the prison of time: always in sleep, but often in our richest waking hours. The mind may traverse years in moments, leap back and forth in the blink of an eye. The impressionist wandering in time is sustained throughout *A Personal Record,* although memory is framed by two beginnings: Conrad's work on his first novel and his first encounter, about 1875, with the British merchant marine. Significantly Conrad evokes the winter of 1893-4 in his first chapter, 1875 in his beautiful last one.

Third, A Personal Record, in common with the other autobiographical classics I have cited, achieves its finest effects through the juxtaposition of vivid specific memory and cool meditative comment. "An imaginative and exact rendering of authentic memories may serve worthily that spirit of piety toward all things human which sanctions the conceptions of a writer of tales, and the emotions of a man reviewing his own experience." *Imaginative and yet exact and authentic, exactness serving piety, piety sanctioning conceptions—A Personal Record* is rich in grand sweeping generalizations which may, as here, embody challenging paradoxes. But the marvelously concrete, dramatic and immediate again and again interrupt these distancing abstractions. Thus for three intensely personal experiences recorded: the five-year-old child returning with his mother to political exile, after a three-month leave; the ship officer encountering the real-life model of the central figure of his first novel; the young adventurer in the dark nighttime company of Marseilles pilots, about to lay his hand on the side of a British ship for the first time.

Unforgettable, for the reader as for Conrad, are the police captain of the district, and the grandmother all in black, and the "elongated, *bizarre*, shabby traveling-carriage with four post-horses," but most particularly the governess urging him not to forget his French. In very few words both a person and a loving relationship are created:

> the good, ugly Mlle. Durand, the governess, with her black eyebrows meeting over a short, thick nose, and a complexion like pale brown paper. Of all the eyes turned toward the carriage, her good-natured eyes only were dropping tears, and it was her sobbing voice alone that broke the silence with an appeal to me: *"N'oublie pas ton français, mon chéri."*

The first encounter with his first novelistic protagonist is as vivid. Almayer, "clad simply in flapping pajamas of cretonne pattern (enormous flowers with yellow petals on a disagreeable blue ground)," has come to meet a ship bringing him a pony. But the pony itself testifies to the novelist's impulse to vivify even the humblest reality:

> His little hoofs thundered tremendously; he plunged and reared. He had tossed his mane and his forelock into a state of amazing wildness, he dilated his nostrils, bits of foam flecked his broad little chest, his eyes blazed. He was something under eleven hands; he was fierce, terrible, angry,

warlike; he said ha! ha! distinctly; he raged and thumped—and sixteen able-bodied kalashes stood round him like disconcerted nurses round a spoiled and passionate child.

So too for the unforgotten evening on which the young would-be seaman hears the voice of a British sailor for the first time, as a small boatload of pilots moves through the night outside the Vieux Port of Marseilles, looking for work. Conrad evokes from among them an old retired pilot who as a child had seen Napoleon returning from Elba:

> one grandfather, with a shaved, bony face and a great beak of a nose, had a cloak with a hood which made him look in our midst like a cowled monk being carried off goodness knows where by that silent company of seamen—quiet enough to be dead. . . I had seen and examined one of the buttons of his old brown, patched coat, the only brass button of the miscellaneous lot, flat and thin, with the words *Équipages de ligne* engraved on it. That sort of button, I believe, went out with the last of the French Bourbons. "I preserved it from the time of my navy service," he explained, nodding rapidly his frail, vulture-like head.

Appropriately, for this night that anticipates his career as British seaman and ship's officer, Conrad renders in a single sentence both the humble labor and the romantic glamor of life at sea:

> With a quick rattle of blocks and one single silky swish, the sail is filled by a little breeze keen enough to have come straight down from the frozen moon, and the boat, after the clatter of the

141

> hauled-in sweeps, seems to stand at rest, sur-
> rounded by a mysterious whispering so faint and
> unearthly that it may be the rustling of the bril-
> liant, overpowering moon-rays breaking like a
> rain-shower upon the hard, smooth, shadowless
> sea.

The close view and the long, the immediate moment and vast avenues of time, the glistening particular and the magesterial abstraction—Conrad was not entirely wrong in saying that all his art lay in perspective. Fair enough, if we define perspective broadly enough.

Such is my affectionate response to *A Personal Record* in 1988. My response thirty years before, in *Conrad the Novelist*, was somewhat less personal and somewhat more academic, though not really very different. It seems only proper, since that book is out of print, to append without alteration what I said then:

The "real" Conrad is doubtless as irrecoverable as the "real" Hardy or the "real" Gide. Of the shadowy being we can begin to recover, an obvious trait of temperament is an evasiveness bent on keeping distances. It is a trait too complex to be dismissed as mere pride and aristocratic aloofness. The evasiveness of the prefaces to the collected works is notorious: it is coy, clearly embarrassed, and at times rather tiresome. Conrad was wise not to supply too many clues to novels which are mysteries for the reader to explore. But also he obviously felt himself in a new and improper relationship to the public, in these prefaces, and protected his privacy as best he could. *This much you shall know of me, and no more.* Gide too was slippery and elusive, but he made a great and even compulsive effort to expose the secrets of his sexual and artistic life. With Conrad as with Faulkner we feel an equally strong reluctance to talk about personal matters. Except of course in fiction! Thus certain episodes remain for the biographer very dark indeed: Conrad's Marseilles adventure and his brief visit to South America or Faulkner's wartime experience. The preposterous inventions of some Faulkner interviews suggest a humorous disdain for a public that had so long misread his work. There may be some of this in Conrad too, who granted almost no interviews, and whose professions of respect for the general public are wholly contradicted by his letters. But in both writers the object finally to be circled and concealed may be, simply, the self.

This evasiveness, however irritating to the biographer, can be one of the foundations of a high art. And Conrad's *A Personal Record* (1912) is a true work of art. It proposes to describe the beginnings of the two great adventures: the initiation to the sea, the initiation to the life of a writer. But the narrative begins with his writing of the tenth chapter of *Almayer's Folly* while landlocked in Rouen aboard the *Adowa* (which was to be his last ship) in the winter of 1893-94. And it ends with his first momentary contact with a British ship, in 1874 or 1875. Between this beginning which was really an ending and this end which was truly a beginning Conrad's memory flows freely in time and space: over his childhood and Polish heritage, over his first meeting with one Kaspar Almayer, over certain later experiences as a writer. The autobiography exploits, that is, the now perfected technique of impressionistic fiction; and the "free" flow of memory is in fact beautifully controlled to achieve certain startling transitions, and to play intimately with the sensibilities of readers. It is one of Conrad's most subtly and most deliberately constructed books. And it suggests that the technique chosen for a most evasive personal record was temperamentally suited to the writer of very personal novels. The experiments in a new novelistic form also respected a deep psychic need to control and modify one's distance from experience.

"Even before the most seductive reveries I have remained mindful of that sobriety of interior life, that asceticism of sentiment, in which alone the naked form of truth, such as one conceives it, such as one feels it, can be rendered without shame." In this and a few more such passages Conrad reminds us of the great contradiction of his life: the dreamer, adventurer, audacious seaman, and innovating subjective writer was also a cool rationalist, political conservative, and withdrawn spectator. As factual autobiography *A Personal Record* is exceptionally evasive—which makes it all the truer to the temperament it proposes to express. Doubtless it comes closest to essential conflicts and anxieties in the pages concerning Poland. One paradox is less severe than it might seem to certain modern readers, though more severe than Conrad pretended: that this conservative satirist of revolution and critic of social-democrat visionaries was the son of Apollo Korzeniowski, leader of the Red faction in the Polish uprising of 1863. Conrad makes short shrift of the critic who called him "son of a Revolutionist," but there is some evidence that the father was in fact more revolutionary and more visionary than many of his colleagues.

A Personal Record contains affectionate evocations of adventurous forbears, as of the grand-uncle Nicholas who during the Napoleonic retreat from Moscow ate Lithuanian dog. He did it, Conrad comments, *pro patria;* "in that light it appears a sweet and decorous meal." The whimsical remark is important, and suggests that the paradoxes of Conrad are indeed similar to those of Faulkner—the two men belonging to an aristocratic tradition which yet professed sympathy for the underprivileged of the earth; recalling with amused envy and pride the fantastic military exploits of ancestors; belonging to lands that had been invaded and brutally occupied; and now watching with disdain a degraded present and the manipulation of the masses by propaganda. The key to the Faulkner social ethic is an aristocratic *noblesse oblige.* And as Faulkner falls into an exalted breathless rhetoric when making certain large affirmations, so too

144

does Conrad in "Prince Roman," one of his most affirmative stories, whose subject is literally *noblesse oblige.* "But as soon as he found his voice he thanked God aloud for letting him live long enough to see the descendant of the illustrious family in its youngest generation give an example *coram Gentibus* of the love of his country and of valor in the field." These are the tones and this is the running rhythm of Conrad when he is deeply moved— whether in enthusiasm or contempt*—and his biographer would do well to attend to all such passages. Prince Roman, whom Conrad had seen as a child, led his score of cholera-ravaged soldiers to a fortress where the last stand of the 1831 revolution (the narrator himself uses the word) was made. And even Conrad must recognize that such action looks like the fanaticism he professes to abhor:

But fanaticism is human. Man has adored ferocious divinities. There is ferocity in every passion, even in love itself. The religion of undying hope resembles the mad cult of despair, of death, of annihilation. The difference lies in the moral motive springing from the secret needs and the unexpressed aspiration of the believers. It is only to vain men that all is vanity; and all is deception only to those who have never been sincere with themselves.

---

* The rhythm and at times the rhetoric are similar to those of (especially in France) the proclamation and manifesto. The issue of Polish nationality provoked this style even in a cablegram of 1920. I quote the cablegram only as far as the first comma:

"For Poles the sense of duty and the imperishable feeling of nationality preserved in the hearts and defended by the hands of their immediate ancestors in open struggles against the might of three powers and in indomitable defence of crushing oppression for more than a hundred years is sufficient inducement to assist in reconstructing the independent dignity and usefulness of the reborn republic . . ." (G. Jean-Aubry, *Joseph Conrad: Life and Letters* [2 vols. New York, 1927], II, 239).

145

Pro patria; and rationalism has its limits. The analogy with Faulkner is further significant, since Faulkner has not left the South. In *The Polish Heritage of Joseph Conrad* Gustav Morf insists too literally on the guilt-feelings attached to the "desertion" of Poland and to British naturalization. The echoes and reflections he finds in the novels seem too direct and undisguised. But the charge of a kind of desertion is one the young Conrad had to face in 1874 and later, and it is the most uncomfortable matter with which *A Personal Record* must deal:

> . . . for why should I, the son of a land which such men as these have turned up with their plough-shares and bedewed with their blood, undertake the pursuit of fantastic meals of salt junk and hard tack upon the wide seas? On the kindest view it seems an unanswerable question. Alas! I have the conviction that there are men of unstained recti-tude who are ready to murmur scornfully the word desertion. Thus the taste of innocent adventure may be made bitter to the palate. The part of the inexplicable should be allowed for in appraising the conduct of men in a world where no explana-tion is final. No charge of faithlessness ought to be lightly uttered.

> But for a boy between fifteen and sixteen, sensi-tive enough, in all conscience, the commotion of his little world had seemed a very considerable thing indeed. So considerable that, absurdly enough, the echoes of it linger to this day. I catch myself in hours of solitude and retrospect meeting arguments and charges made thirty-five years ago by voices now for ever still; finding things to say that an assailed boy could not have found, simply because of the mysteriousness of his impulses to himself. I understood no more than the people

who called upon me to explain myself. There was no precedent. I verily believe mine was the only case of a boy of my nationality and antecedents taking a, so to speak, standing jump out of his racial surroundings and associations.

One more passage takes us very close to the heart of this elusive book, and to the determination of Conrad as seaman. It refers to the sea appreciations given him by various captains:

It seems that it is for these few bits of paper, headed by the names of a few ships and signed by the names of a few Scots and English shipmasters, that I have faced the astonished indignation, the mockeries and the reproaches of a sort hard to bear for a boy of fifteen; that I have been charged with the want of patriotism, the want of sense, and the want of heart too; that I went through agonies of self-conflict and shed secret tears not a few, and had the beauties of the Furca Pass spoiled for me, and have been called an "incorrigible Don Quixote," in allusion to the book-born madness of the knight. For that spoil. They rustle, those bits of paper—some dozen of them in all . . . I do not know whether I have been a good seaman, but I know I have been a very faithful one.

"Those who read me know my conviction that the world, the temporal world, rests on a few very simple ideas; so simple that they must be as old as the hills. It rests notably, among others, on the idea of Fidelity."

These sentences, coming from a writer so complex and subtle, and who dramatized betrayal so magnificently, have astonished various readers. But in a life whose two great events were "jumps"—the departure from Poland in

147

1874, the quitting of the sea in 1894—the obligation to prove one's fidelity was great. So too was the obligation to succeed in a chosen hard task.

—ALBERT J. GUERARD